The Symbolic Imagination

11 October 2001

For Roger Haight —
"May all the stars
hang bright above your
dwelling"!
With all best
blessings —

Bob Buth, S.J.

STUDIES IN RELIGION AND LITERATURE
John L. Mahoney, series editor

The Symbolic Imagination

Coleridge and the Romantic Tradition

SECOND EDITION

J. ROBERT BARTH, S.J.

Fordham University Press
New York
2001

LC 2001033031
ISBN 0–8232–2112–1 hardcover
ISBN 0–8232–2113–X paperback
Studies in Religion and Literature, No. 3
ISSN 1096–6692

Library of Congress Cataloging in Publication Data

Barth, J. Robert.
    The symbolic imagination : Coleridge and the romantic
tradition / J. Robert Barth.—Second ed.
        p. cm.—(Studies in religion and literature ; no. 3)
    Includes bibliographical references and index.
    ISBN 0-8232-2112-1 (hardcover)—
    ISBN 0-8232-2113-X (pbk.)
        1. Coleridge, Samuel Taylor, 1772–1834—Symbolism.
2. Symbolism in literature. 3. Romanticism—England.
I. Title. II. Studies in religion and literature (Fordham
University Press) ; no. 3.

PR4487.S95 B3   2001
821′.7—dc21   2001033031

Printed in the United States of America

To
Philip C. Rule, S.J.
brother and friend

CONTENTS

SERIES EDITOR'S INTRODUCTION

It has been more than twenty years since Princeton University Press published J. Robert Barth's *The Symbolic Imagination: Coleridge and the Romantic Tradition*. The book, praised by a range of distinguished reviewers with differing critical orientations, has been out of print and difficult to get for some time. Because of its strong emphasis on the religious dimension in Coleridge's aesthetic theory, it seemed appropriate that Fordham University Press consider it as the third volume in its developing Religion and Literature Series. And Barth, a continuing presence in Romantic studies and in the discourse interested in connections between art and religion, was eager to revisit his 1977 volume and, while not altering his basic argument, to develop it more fully and bring it into the notable contemporary dialogue on Coleridge's theory of imagination. Our reviewers agreed that this new and expanded edition fulfilled his expectations.

This volume, then, is a notably fresh and engaging study. Barth's distinction between the eighteenth-century "poetry of reference" and the new Romantic "poetry of encounter," and his strong emphasis on symbol as the agent of encounter that draws us into experience, remain his vital starting-points. And two new chapters, both revealing his continuing reflection, lecturing, and writing on the subjects, explore in even greater depth the theological foundation of Coleridge's idea of symbol and what he calls the scriptural dimension of his imagination. For Barth, the imagination and its symbolic renderings are at the heart of the questing spirit of Romanticism.

What we have here is a "new life" for a superior contribution to Coleridge students and to the rapidly developing field of religious critical discourse.

JOHN L. MAHONEY

ABBREVIATIONS

BL	*Biographia Literaria*, ed. Engell and Bate
CL	*Collected Letters*, ed. Griggs
FR	*The Friend*, ed. Rooke
LL	*Lectures 1808–1819 On Literature*, ed. Foakes
LS	*Lay Sermons*, ed. White
TT	*Table Talk*, ed. Woodring

PREFACE TO THE FIRST EDITION

No book ever happens in a vacuum—least of all, I am tempted to add, a book on Coleridge. The studies of Coleridge in recent years have been so many and so various that one almost despairs, at times, of keeping up with them. One should perhaps feel a bit embarrassed at adding to their number even such a modest offering as this.

And yet there has been need, I think, of serious attention to the matter of symbol in Coleridge. I came at the problem originally in the context of my earlier study, *Coleridge and Christian Doctrine*, but have since come to realize more fully that it stands at the heart of his whole intellectual endeavor, whether in poetry or criticism or philosophy. This book will not solve all the problems, perhaps not even articulate them all, but it will at least make a beginning.

In addition, I have extended the range of the study beyond Coleridge himself—and Wordsworth, his example *par excellence* of the poetry of the symbolic imagination—to make certain generalizations about Romantic poetry itself. I have been led to do so because it has seemed to me that the symbolic, and hence (in a Coleridgean view) the religious, aspects of Romantic poets have too often been ignored or distorted, and that Coleridge's views on the religious character of symbol can shed considerable light on them.

Acknowledging personal debts and kindnesses is always a happy task. First of all, I must thank the staffs of two libraries for their generous assistance: the Harvard College Library and the Ellis Library of the University of Missouri-Columbia. Their cooperation has been unstinting. I am also grateful to the Berg Collection of the New York Public Library for permission to quote two passages from a still unpublished Coleridge notebook.

I am pleased to thank the National Endowment for the

Humanities and the American Council of Learned Societies for summer grants, several years ago, to begin study toward the writing of this book. I have also been assisted by a Harvard Faculty Research Grant and by a grant from the Research Council of the Graduate School, University of Missouri-Columbia.

The editors of *Studies in Romanticism* have graciously allowed me to use, as the second chapter of this book, an essay that first appeared in that journal. I am grateful for their kind permission.

I must add, too, my thanks for the assistance of an impeccable and indefatigable typist, Mrs. Martha Robinson, and for the capable assistance of Susan Darley with the work of indexing.

My debts to colleagues are many. Professors W. Jackson Bate and David Perkins of Harvard University and Professor Philip C. Rule, S.J., of the University of Detroit, all read an early version of the manuscript and gave me the benefit not only of encouragement but of extensive and helpful criticism. My personal debts to these three friends are of long duration, and go far beyond the making of this book.

I would like to add a special word of thanks to Professor Thomas McFarland of the City University of New York Graduate Center, with whom I have talked much, these past several years, on Coleridge and Coleridgeana.

Finally, my colleagues at the University of Missouri have been generous in their encouragement and support, as well as in their counsel. I must mention especially Professor Howard Hinkel, my colleague in Romantic studies, and Professors Haskell Hinnant and Catherine Neal Parke, eighteenth-century scholars, who read all or part of the manuscript and offered valuable suggestions for its improvement. To them, and to my other colleagues in Columbia, I am deeply grateful for their conversation and counsel, but especially for their friendship.

Columbia, Missouri   J. R. B.
January 1976

PREFACE TO THE
SECOND EDITION

Since the publication of the original edition of this book, several new volumes in the *Collected Coleridge* have appeared: James Engell and W. Jackson Bate's magisterial edition of *Biographia Literaria* (1983); R. A. Foakes's exacting edition of the difficult material in *Lectures 1808–1819 on Literature* (1987); Carl Woodring's fine version of *Table Talk* (1990); and the long-awaited *Aids to Reflection*, meticulously and sensitively edited by John Beer (1993). For this new edition of *The Symbolic Imagination*, references to Coleridge's works have been updated accordingly.

Besides several textual changes here and there throughout the book, an introduction discussing the scholarship of the past two decades on imagination and symbol has been added to this new edition, along with two new chapters. Chapter 1, an earlier version of which first appeared in *Studies in the Literary Imagination* (1986), offers a theological foundation for Coleridge's theory of symbol, which is then considered more specifically under the rubric of "sacrament" in chapter 2; I am grateful to the editors of the journal for permission to use this material here. Chapter 6, on Coleridge's "scriptural imagination," turns our attention from an application of his theory in Wordsworth's poetry and his own, to its application in the poetry of sacred scripture. The original version of this essay appeared in the *Festschrift* for W. Jackson Bate, *Coleridge, Keats, and the Imagination*.

Happily, with the passing of years, occasions for gratitude mount up as one's circle of friends and colleagues grows. My debts, not only for work on this book but for helping me to continue a scholarly life through more than a decade of academic administration, are many and varied.

Boston College is blessed with unusual library resources. The Thomas P. O'Neill, Jr. Library has consistently provided a high level of support and professionalism; Jerome Yavarkovsky and his staff offer remarkably dedicated and personal service. In the same way, the John J. Burns Library of Rare Books and Special Collections, under the direction of Robert K. O'Neill, provides us with both service and inspiration. We are all in their debt.

To "the ladies of Gasson Hall"—Donna McHale, Margery Ferry, and Louise Stewart—I am deeply grateful for the generous support and loving friendship of many years; and I am pleased to recognize the splendid work of my research assistant, Matthew VanWinkle, who has brought to this project an extraordinary level of care, scholarship, and professionalism.

I am grateful to Boston College, and especially to the Research Fund of the James P. McIntyre Chair, for an extended research opportunity following eleven years as Dean of the College of Arts and Sciences. "We must be still and still moving."

For almost twenty-five years I have been fortunate enough to be part of the lecture staff at the Wordsworth Summer Conference in Grasmere. The circle of discourse and the friendships of that remarkable annual gathering have been an important part of my life. To the immediate purpose, two chapters of the earlier version of this book and the two new chapters in this edition had their first presentation in Grasmere; the responses and criticism of colleagues there, and in subsequent discussions, have undoubtedly strengthened them. Over the years John Beer, Frederick Burwick, Marilyn Gaull, Molly Lefebure, Thomas McFarland, Anya Taylor, Jonathan Wordsworth—and many others too numerous to name—have offered suggestions and criticism, support and friendship; and Sylvia Wordsworth has, of course, been for all of us a warm and gracious presence.

John L. Mahoney, my devoted friend and wise colleague

in the English department at Boston College—with his dear wife, Ann—has supported and advised me in every project I have undertaken. My nineteenth-century colleagues Judith Wilt and Alan Richardson have also supported me by their friendship and inspired me by their own work. Philip C. Rule, S.J., of the English department of the College of the Holy Cross, has been for more years than either of us cares to admit a treasured friend and good counselor; the continuing dedication of this book to him bears witness to the durability of this friendship.

Other important personal obligations call out for recognition. The Jesuits of the Roberts House community have been truly brothers and friends; in times of joy and times of sadness they have been there, to celebrate or to support. Sister Maryan Russo, C.I.J., has been for many years a blessed gift and, as a beloved uncle used to say, "an anchor to windward." Finally, my family has been a source of loving strength: my brothers and sisters, with all their children, have been close and caring; my indomitable father has taught us more than he knows; and the memory of my mother is a warm embrace for us all. We still miss the wise and wry presence of our brother Karl, but—as the little girl insisted—"Sir, we are seven"!

To all of these, and so many others, I can only say: "A spring of love gushed from my heart, / And I blessed them unaware."

Chestnut Hill, Massachusetts   J.R.B.
January 16, 2000

Past and Present: A Prologue

SCHOLARSHIP IN A FIELD as complex as that of Coleridge studies does not stand still. In the more than two decades since the original edition of this book was published, work on Coleridge's theology and religious thought and on his views of the imagination has continued unabated, and it has been for the most part rich and illuminating. My own continued reflection on Coleridge's "symbolic imagination" has taken place within the context of this larger Coleridgean enterprise. Thus, an overview of some of the notable contributions of others may be appropriate and useful.

Three years after the publication of *The Symbolic Imagination*, a book appeared that provided a useful historical perspective on Coleridge's thinking about symbol: Jadwiga Swiatecka's *The Idea of the Symbol: Some Nineteenth-Century Comparisons with Coleridge* (1980).[1] Perhaps because it is not uniformly strong—there are weaknesses in both style and substance—it has not received the attention it deserves. However, several chapters are excellent and still worth rereading. The chapter on Coleridge himself, "The Term 'Symbol' and Its Cognates in the Thought of Coleridge," is thoughtful and lucid. In particular, her discussion of the crucial distinction between allegory and symbol allows her to expound very well one of the central themes of the book: that in Coleridge's thought symbol implies a whole, strongly developed view of the world. As Swiatecka puts it, "Symbols . . . are, for Coleridge, the visible tips of

---

[1] *The Idea of the Symbol: Some Nineteenth-Century Comparisons with Coleridge* (Cambridge, 1980). Some of the remarks that follow on this book are taken from my review in *Studies in Romanticism*, 21 (1982), 703–707.

an ontological iceberg." More specifically, "to say that 'this is a symbol' in the Coleridgean sense, is also to make a statement about the structure of each component of the universe, and about the inter-relationship between all created things and their creator" (p. 59).

Among the Victorian thinkers Swiatecka discusses, she is particularly persuasive in her discussion of Carlyle, arguing—contrary to the position I take in chapter 7 of this book—that the obvious similarities between Coleridge and Carlyle on the nature of symbol are more than counterbalanced by the significant differences. And what is most essentially different are their views of the relationship between the created world and God. Although both of them "could, and did, speak of the universe as a symbol of God" (p. 87), Carlyle's Calvinist background left him with a view of God as "distant, in a Heaven to which some may look forward, rather than present in history and time" (p. 81). The visible world, therefore, is for Carlyle much more "shadow" than reality (pp. 81–82), and visible symbol much more a "concealment" than a revelation. For Carlyle, "the symbol is opaque rather than transcendent" (p. 86). In Swiatecka's view, symbol for Carlyle shares in the corruption of the world: it can shadow forth a higher world but cannot embody it; the symbol cannot be "one with that which it symbolizes" (p. 87).

Almost equally convincingly, Swiatecka argues for significant differences in emphasis between Coleridge and Newman on the relationship between God and the world, and therefore on the nature of symbol. For Newman the world of visible reality, while it mediates the presence of God to man, remains primarily a veil through which God is glimpsed—"the transcendent God allowing himself to be glimpsed through, but beyond, the phenomenal world" (p. 115). For Coleridge, the world is more truly sacramental, more truly an "embodiment of God's presence"; his view of symbol expresses "God's immanence in the world, and the consequent capacity of that world to be, in itself, revelatory" (p. 115).

Coleridge is placed in an even broader historical context in James Engell's magisterial *The Creative Imagination: Enlightenment to Romanticism* (1981).[2] His treatment of Coleridge on imagination is the last and climactic chapter, following twenty closely argued chapters demonstrating that "the idea of the imagination, as understood in the Romantic period and as we still understand it today, was actually the creation of the eighteenth century" (p. vii) and tracing its development from the empiricism of Hobbes and Locke to the idealism of Coleridge. The theological foundation of Coleridge's view of imagination is demonstrated with clarity and force, particularly in his excellent discussion of "the constitutive property of ideas," which "leads to a swift conclusion: since the material world and human reason are governed by the same laws or ideas, imagination not only unifies the mind in one process but also *is* (or is at least a part of) the creative force of eternal reason as it works in the universe" (p. 341).

Another important contribution by Engell—together with the late Walter Jackson Bate—is the long-anticipated edition, with a splendid hundred-page introductory essay, of the *Biographia Literaria*.[3] The entire Editors' Introduction is worthy of attention and reflection, but for the present purpose the sections on imagination (pp. lxxxi–xcvii) and on the fancy/imagination distinction (pp. xcvii–civ) are especially significant. Engell and Bate are excellent in discussing the relation of imagination to symbol, and their perspective is appropriately broad. The imagination "creates and communicates through symbols. Its medium, whether in perception, art, or philosophy, is symbolic in the widest sense of the word, for a symbol embodies an objective externality, a definite shape or sign of recognition that becomes identified with the internal processes of mind and feeling that it represents" (p. lxxxiii).

---

[2] *The Creative Imagination: Enlightenment to Romanticism* (Cambridge, Mass., 1981).

[3] *Biographia Literaria*, ed. James Engell and W. Jackson Bate, vol. 7 of *The Collected Works of Samuel Taylor Coleridge*, ed. Kathleen Coburn, 2 vols., Bollingen Series 75 (Princeton, 1983).

But Engell and Bate's view is as deep as it is broad; they probe carefully and subtly the religious dimensions of imagination and symbol, and conclude: "Coleridge came to believe that our symbols of perception are constitutive with nature; they truly represent the ideal form and divine power responsible for creating nature and nature's laws" (p. lxxxiii). "By penetrating the spirit of nature and approaching the source of all creativity, the speculative intellect leads to God, and philosophy to religion." And so, in short, "the final significance is religious" (p. xciv). Thus, for Coleridge, "our intuitions, our philosophic imaginations, meet the divine in a middle ground where the divine chooses to appear to us" (p. xcvi).

In 1982 a work appeared in English whose aim was to place the "symbol" in a longer and broader perspective than had recently been attempted: Tzvetan Todorov's *Theories of the Symbol.*[4] Although Todorov denies that he is dealing with "all the theories of the symbol [or] even perhaps with the most important among them" (p. 10), the book is a remarkably ambitious and successful history of symbol from Augustine (including the ancient Greek and Roman sources that influenced him) to Roman Jakobson. In spite of the wide range of its interest, however, the book "is organized around a period of crisis which coincides with the end of the eighteenth century," since "a radical change in ways of thinking about the symbol occurred in this period" (p. 10), the change from a "classic" to a "romantic" view of symbol—a change that involved a shift from the priority of rhetoric to the primacy of aesthetics. As Todorov says of the transition from the eighteenth to the nineteenth century, "aesthetics begins precisely where rhetoric ends" (p. 111).

The heart of Todorov's argument is found in chapter 6 ("The Romantic Crisis"), in which he traces clearly and cogently the rise of the distinction between allegory and symbol. For, he writes, "nowhere does the meaning of 'symbol'

---

[4] *Theories of the Symbol,* trans. Catherine Porter (Ithaca, N.Y., 1982). The original French version, *Theorie du Symbole,* appeared in 1977.

appear so clearly as in the opposition between symbol and allegory—an opposition invented by the romantics and one that allows them to oppose themselves to all other viewpoints" (p. 199). Although Todorov's thesis is grounded almost entirely in the German Romantics—Coleridge is mentioned only twice, and only in passing—his argument sheds considerable light on Coleridge's thought through its antecedents. Future scholars of British Romantic thought will need to take serious account of this splendid work.

One of the most suggestive books on imagination in recent years is Thomas McFarland's *Originality and Imagination* (1985),[5] in which the author—out of his immense store of learning—traces from Plato to Coleridge the evolution of the idea of "soul" into the Enlightenment and finally Romantic idea of imagination. He argues acutely and persuasively that, with the decline of acceptance of belief in the soul, imagination came to take its place as a means of articulating the relationship between the human and the divine.

As is sometimes the case with this brilliant theorist, there is much to argue with, for McFarland's skepticism sometimes has the effect of limiting his openness to theological argument and insight. For example, his view that "the theologian today who actually believes in God is a *rara avis* indeed" (p. ix) suggests a limited acquaintance with the theological world of discourse; and his contention that St. Paul (in 1 Cor. 15:13–19) "hedges" the immortality of the soul and the "consequent validity of Christian faith" (pp. ix–x) is clearly based on an incomplete reading of the text.

Having said this, though, one can only be impressed and enlightened by McFarland's remarkable grasp of philosophical issues and intellectual history and by his ultimate hopefulness even in the throes of deep skepticism. On Coleridge he is superb; few scholars today can match his range and depth of learning. As McFarland traces the decline of the idea of "soul" in Western thought, he delineates brilliantly the rise of imagination, culminating in his masterful discus-

---

[5] *Originality and Imagination* (Baltimore, 1985).

sion of Coleridge on imagination. His final chapter, on "The Higher Function of Imagination," is subtle and utterly convincing, as he traces the "ascending ladder" from fancy to imagination, a ladder that "rises to Godhead itself, to the 'infinite I AM.' The thrust is inexorably upward, toward the most honorific conceptions the mind can entertain. It is this upward movement, even more than the attempt to discriminate its exact mode of operation, that typifies the Romantic concern with imagination." In Coleridge and Wordsworth, as well as in Romantic thought generally, "imagination is persistently hailed as functioning in the same spiritual realm as does the idea of soul" (pp. 149–150).

Since Coleridge's day, McFarland sees the symbolic dimensions of imagination, which operated so strongly for Coleridge and his age, fading in power for the modern sensibility, even as imagination itself still lives: "Symbol, though once the very heart of Christian theology, is today a conception largely limited to literary theory, and somewhat passé even there. . . . But imagination is still vital, incommensurable, and current." The idea of symbol may have lost its power to enliven us, but "imagination still is as mysterious as it is powerful" (p. 198). This is enough, McFarland argues eloquently, to give us hope. Imagination ("and its cognate, originality") are, even today, "defenses for the hopes and dignity of the human" (p. 199).

My own argument throughout this book will be otherwise, contending that imagination and symbol cannot be separated, any more than the water can from the fountain, and that both retain—even in what some consider these dark Derridean times—their power to touch and move us. At the same time, McFarland's learning and eloquence challenge us to make our arguments with as much sensitivity and passion as he has demonstrated.

Another brilliant study of Coleridge's view of imagination was published in the same year as McFarland's book: Jonathan Wordsworth's essay "The Infinite I AM: Coleridge and the Ascent of Being" (1985).[6] In some thirty pages of close argument, grounded in a perceptive reading of Coleridge and his sources, Wordsworth mines magnificently the famous closing paragraphs of Chapter XIII of the *Biographia Literaria.*

Against the common view that the secondary imagination is the higher faculty, he argues—as I do in this book—that the primary imagination is, in fact, the higher human faculty, because it participates directly in the divine power. Coleridge's sentence is of course well known: "The primary IMAGINATION I hold to be the living Power and prime Agent of all human Perception, and as a repetition in the finite mind of the eternal act of creation in the infinite I AM." Jonathan Wordsworth's analysis of these words is memorable: "The sentence is magnificently affirmative. Stress in both halves falls on the adjectives. Those in the first could hardly be more positive: '*living* Power', '*prime* Agent', '*all* human Perception'; while in the second there is an escalation, 'finite'—'eternal'—'infinite', that speaks for itself. Whatever its purpose, the prose exultantly proclaims an incarnation of the eternal in the finite, a personal reenactment of God's original, and endlessly continuous, moment of self-naming" (p. 24).

As Jonathan Wordsworth makes clear, "it is not Coleridge but his critics who have been preoccupied with the poetic imagination. The game of Pick-your-own-German-philosopher has led to Kant, Fichte, Tetens, Schelling being ridden like hobby-horses through the pages of *Biographia*, and has distracted attention from the fact that imagination is for Coleridge an act of faith" (p. 46). And again: "Coleridge is at all times a Christian thinker. Philosophy is not a pastime, or an intellectual pursuit; it is a means of understanding the nature of God, and the nature of man's relation

---

[6] "The Infinite I AM: Coleridge and the Ascent of Being," in *Coleridge's Imagination: Essays in Memory of Pete Laver*, ed. Richard Gravil, Lucy Newlyn, and Nicholas Roe (Cambridge, 1985).

to God" (pp. 31–32). Thus, "in his definitions [Coleridge] scaled downwards from the primary at the top to the fancy at the bottom because he was thinking in terms of human achievement, and the primary in its full potential showed man at his closest to God. The primary definition is a statement of faith" (p. 48). Compared with the primary imagination, "the secondary can only be inferior: it is a merely human faculty, not an interpenetration of the divine" (p. 49).

I have only one important demurrer from Jonathan Wordsworth's view: he argues, cogently but not for me persuasively, that the *Biographia Literaria* is "a pantheist work, dependent upon Schelling" (p. 44), but that this pantheism is not necessarily incompatible with orthodox Christian belief (p. 39). In my view, Coleridge never—for all his flirtations with pantheism—succumbed to its charms. As I argue in chapter 2 of this book, and later in chapter 6, it is Coleridge's concepts of "consubstantiality" and "translucence" that allow him to affirm the closest possible unity between the human and the divine, while still affirming their essential distinction. Both in action and in being, I shall contend—with Coleridge, I believe—that God and man may be distinct from each other without being separate.

Jonathan Wordsworth's essay remains, however, one of the most important studies of Coleridge on imagination in recent years, and it deserves the most serious attention by anyone who takes up these issues.

About 1985, Christine Gallant invited a group of Romantic scholars—including John Beer, Thomas McFarland, and Brian Wilkie—to contribute to a special issue of the journal *Studies in the Literary Imagination* on Coleridge's theory of imagination.[7] Ultimately, that splendid issue was expanded, with additional contributions from several other distinguished Romanticists—Jerome Christensen, John Grant, Anthony John Harding, Laurence Lockridge, Paul Magnu-

---

[7] "Coleridge's Theory of the Imagination as Critical Method Today," special issue of *Studies in the Literary Imagination*, 19, No. 2 (Fall 1986).

son, Jean-Pierre Mileur, Raimonda Modiano, David Simpson, Peter L. Thorsley, Jr., Kathleen M. Wheeler, and Susan Wolfson—into a remarkable collection of essays, *Coleridge's Theory of Imagination Today*.[8] The range of the essays is very broad, both in attitude and in methodology. For example, as Gallant points out, the contributors to the original issue "ranged from the fervent apologist J. Robert Barth, S.J., to the considerably less sanguine Norman Fruman" (p. ix). The sixteen essays are almost evenly divided between approaches to Coleridge's theory of imagination and detailed studies of his "praxis," the application of his theory to practical criticism.

Although the essays were written independently of one another, a fascinating dialogue does emerge, in which important differences of viewpoint—whether in the interpretation of Coleridge's theory, in judgments about its value, or in the methodologies by which it is applied in practice—play off interestingly against one another. Not only is this volume an extraordinarily useful and important collection of approaches to Coleridge, but these essays also, as Gallant very properly points out, "illustrate to varying degrees most of the critical approaches being taken today," by showing "the different ways in which the imagination may 'diffuse and dissolve' the text to recreate a new order" (p. xii). This book remains an important landmark in the ongoing study of Coleridge's thought.

It is not only literary critics who have studied the religious dimensions of Coleridge's writings on imagination during the past two decades; theologians too have turned to Coleridge's thought. Stephen Happel's book *Coleridge's Religious Imagination* (1983),[9] for example, is worthy of notice. But it is particularly the work of theologian James S. Cutsinger that deserves further attention. In chapter 1 of the

---

[8] *Coleridge's Theory of Imagination Today*, ed. Christine Gallant (New York, 1989).

[9] *Coleridge's Religious Imagination*, Salzburg Studies in English Literature, 3 vols. (Salzburg, 1983).

present book I discuss a pathbreaking essay by Cutsinger, "Coleridgean Polarity and Theological Vision," that appeared in the *Harvard Theological Review*. Several years later, Cutsinger expanded his thinking into a remarkable book, *The Form of Transformed Vision: Coleridge and the Knowledge of God* (1987).[10] Cutsinger's book is superb in its discussion of such central Coleridgean concepts as "interpenetration" and "translucence," as well as symbolism generally, and it traces lucidly and eloquently the history of Coleridge's own "transformed vision."

As Owen Barfield insists in his Foreword to Cutsinger's book, what Coleridge developed was "not a system but a method," and it is "a method that involves imagination, because it is only imagination, and not the abstracting intelligence Coleridge called 'understanding,' which is capable of grasping such fundamentals as polarity, interpenetration, and real symbolism. One of the merits of Cutsinger's book is the thoroughness with which it expounds precisely these three principles; and that is a merit that makes it significant for Coleridge scholarship in general" (pp. x–xi). Cutsinger's splendid book deserves the attention of literary scholars and theologians alike as they ponder the theological and religious implications of Coleridge's thought in years to come.

An intriguing book that takes full advantage of recent studies of imagination and symbol is Jeanie Watson's *Risking Enchantment: Coleridge's Symbolic World of Faery* (1990).[11] She argues persuasively that the fairy tale genre "and the concept of Faery, in general, provide texture, allusion, points of reference, and a symbolic language in Coleridge's poetry throughout his writing career" (p. 1). However, in addition to careful and acute analysis of the fairy tale tradition and Coleridge's use of it, Watson also

---

[10] *The Form of Transformed Vision: Coleridge and the Knowledge of God* (Macon, Ga., 1987).

[11] *Risking Enchantment: Coleridge's Symbolic World of Faery* (Lincoln, Neb., 1990).

explores Coleridge's use of symbol more generally, delineating with learning and insight the philosophical and theological foundations of his view of symbol and of imagination as the symbol-making faculty. As she explains: "In almost every instance, Coleridge's writing, whether poetry or prose exposition, grows out of a set of fundamental assumptions and beliefs about the nature of the universe and the place of the human spirit within that universe. Simply put, the essential belief, underlying all else, is Coleridge's belief in the consubstantial nature of existence. This belief has as a corollary the assumption that if the world is consubstantial, it is also symbolic" (p. 29).

Watson's eloquent first chapter, "The Symbolic World and the World of Faery," is also excellent in its exploration of the "mystery" of how symbol comes to one, whether to the writer or to the listener. "Symbolic knowledge is intuitive," she writes, "given to those who actively wait. It is, one might say, an experience of grace" (p. 36). Her quotations from Coleridge in support of this view are particularly helpful and apt, as, for example, her citation from *Table Talk* (August 24, 1833): "I . . . am inclined to *wait* for the spirit." Watson goes on to gloss this telling phrase: "We will have symbolic knowledge of the mystery of Spirit insofar as we are able to wait for its light, patiently and perceptively, in the still darkness" (p. 37). Here and elsewhere she has caught, I believe, much of the spirit of Coleridge himself.

A *Festschrift* entitled *Coleridge, Keats, and the Imagination: Romanticism and Adam's Dream* (1990)[12] offers essays in honor of the late W. Jackson Bate by a distinguished group of his former students, who explore aspects of the imagination, theoretical and practical, in both Coleridge and Keats. Of particular interest here is the important essay by Thomas McFarland, "Involute and Symbol in the Romantic Imagination," in which he argues strongly and convincingly

---

[12] *Coleridge, Keats, and the Imagination: Romanticism and Adam's Dream,* ed. J. Robert Barth, S.J., and John L. Mahoney (Columbia, Mo., 1990).

against the view of the late Paul De Man that "rather than being superior to allegory . . . symbol is lower than allegory and in fact a conception of little value at all" (p. 39). Unlike De Man, McFarland is acutely aware that "symbol has historically been a conception in the service of theological concerns, and only secondarily in the service of literary concerns" (p. 41). As a result, "such defining attachment of symbol to theology dictates two effects for its use in literary matters. First, it ensures that symbol has an ontological, not a critical, function. Symbol cannot be pressed into service as a tool of criticism: allegory is unravelled by criticism; symbolism is not" (p. 42).

For De Man, McFarland argues, symbol remains only "mystification," while for Coleridge, "symbol's concern for the whole reveals itself as wholly participating in reason itself. Symbol cannot be a mystification. Rather it partakes of the highest cognitive efforts of the mind; its structure is one of cognitive synecdoche, not rhetorical mystification" (p. 51). Thus, McFarland can conclude even more broadly: "For the Romantics, the symbol, which signified the coincidence and fusion of the expressed and the inexpressible, was indeed the last mental entity. It was deeply intertwined with their imaginative emphasis on nature, with their imaginative emphasis on imagination, and with their imaginative emphasis on the infinite" (p. 57).

For Mary Anne Perkins, in her remarkable book *Coleridge's Philosophy: The Logos as Unifying Principle* (1994),[13] symbol is "deeply intertwined" with the Logos in Coleridge's thought. Building on the work of several decades of scholars who have explored the philosophical and theological dimensions of Coleridge's work, she succeeds in articulating beautifully and cogently his "logosophic system" (p. 6). Her foundational chapter 1 ("Logos: The Word") is of particular interest here, since it offers "an exposition of Logos

---

[13] *Coleridge's Philosophy: The Logos as Unifying Principle* (Oxford, 1994).

as the foundation of etymology, linguistic philosophy, of symbol and imagination, and of revelation" (p. 13).

One might go so far as to say that Perkins's discussion of symbol is at the heart of her argument, for she insists that "it is in his theory of symbol that Coleridge most fully expressed his view of the participation of human language in the divine Word." Indeed—as in fact chapter 2 of *The Symbolic Imagination* argues for symbol—Perkins emphasizes that "the initial premiss of his theory of language is an underlying act of faith" (p. 46). In addition, she quite correctly sees Coleridge rejecting "Kant's view of the symbol as representation which cannot put us in touch with noumenal reality. . . . Kant had concluded that 'all our knowledge of God is merely symbol.' Schelling, Goethe, and Coleridge would have thought the word 'merely' a mistake" (p. 47).

For Perkins, the theological implications of symbol are paramount: "For [Coleridge], the symbol both mirrors and participates in the nature of the divine Word, the Logos, the mediator between God and man; there is a consubstantiality in the symbol which echoes the divine *homoousios*" (p. 48). "The symbol," she continues, "unlike the allegory which merely *points* to a unity of appearance and ideality, *is* an inward unity of the objective reality of the universal idea and the subjective apperception of that reality expressed in a particular form" (pp. 48–49).

Perkins's discussion of symbol (especially pp. 47–55) is close and subtle, but even more impressive and helpful is the broad philosophical and theological context in which she places it. This wise and learned book will serve us well as we continue to ponder these and other Coleridgean mysteries.

Ronald C. Wendling's thoughtful and perceptive study, *Coleridge's Progress to Christianity: Experience and Authority in Religious Faith* (1995),[14] traces the evolution of

[14] *Coleridge's Progress to Christianity: Experience and Authority in Religious Faith* (Lewisburg, Pa., 1995).

what he calls Coleridge's "peculiarly empirical transcendentalism" (p. 12). Wendling notes that "in Coleridge, continued awareness of the transcendental, even though it begins and ends in God, occurs only through the sensible world and exists to improve experience of it. His transcendentalism is at once of this earth and demandingly otherworldly" (p. 10).

Although the book is a study of Coleridge's religious development throughout his life, Wendling's reflections on imagination and symbol are particularly important for his discussion of Coleridge's "approach to Trinitarianism" (chapter 6), in which the divine Logos plays a crucial role. He sees the imagination in Coleridge as "the continuously recreating and redeeming divine Logos existing within each human soul. Human creativity repeats the act by which the absolute I AM dissolves its identity with itself and all objects, becomes conscious of them in the Logos, and seeks to attract all back to itself through that creative consciousness." This "redeeming Logos" is "incarnate in all products of the human imagination" (p. 153). Wendling's views on imagination and symbol, especially in the context of Coleridge's religious development, will surely merit further attention in the years to come.

That Coleridge's views on imagination still have power to attract scholars is amply demonstrated by a series of essays over the past few years in *Studies in Romanticism*. In 1991, Ina Lipkowitz wrote on "Inspiration and Poetic Imagination: Samuel Taylor Coleridge,"[15] arguing that his "far greater insight into the role of the creative, or poetic, imagination allowed Coleridge to use his vision of the Bible as 'poetry in the most emphatic sense,' not to minimize its religious truth, but to defend it." She goes on to contend that "in his theory of the symbol, at the heart of his vision of the Bible, both the symbolic poetry and the role of the

---

[15] "Inspiration and Poetic Imagination: Samuel Taylor Coleridge," *Studies in Romanticism*, 30 (1991), 605–631.

imagination that came into prominence in the nineteenth century find their clearest expression" (p. 613). In Lipkowitz's view—as in my own in chapter 6—the Bible had a privileged role in his thinking about the nature and function of imagination. She concludes ringingly: "Without minimizing the role of inspiration, he humanized the prophets and poets of Scripture by locating the source of their sublimity in the imagination, and he correspondingly raised the stature of modern poets who, like Wordsworth, shared the imaginative vision of the biblical writers" (p. 631).

Anthony John Harding, in his essay "Imagination, Patriarchy, and Evil in Coleridge and Heidegger" (1996),[16] takes a darker and more skeptical view of Coleridge on imagination. While admitting that Coleridge's earlier thinking was orthodox in its view of evil as being "not eternal" (p. 10), Harding argues that under the influence of Schelling Coleridge later came to "associate imagination" with "a doctrine that is heterodox in both Judaism and Christianity, the doctrine that good and evil have a common and primordial origin in the division of the light from the darkness" (p. 19). Coleridge might long to recapture the "primordial unity" (p. 26), but cannot find the means to do so.

Two years later in the same journal, Nicholas Reid countered respectfully with his essay "The Satanic Principle in the Later Coleridge's Theory of Imagination" (1998).[17] He concedes that "Harding is right to point to the dark element at the core of the Coleridgean imagination" (p. 277) and that there is "a duality at the heart of the human soul" which "points (as Harding does) to the place of the Satanic element within the human imagination," but "this thesis is not quite as surprising as it first seems, for it merely reflects the fallenness of the human soul" (p. 276). Add to this Coleridge's realization of the "possibility of redemption" (p. 276), and one realizes that Coleridge's views—however

---

[16] "Imagination, Patriarchy, and Evil in Coleridge and Heidegger," *Studies in Romanticism*, 35 (1996), 3–26.

[17] "The Satanic Principle in the Later Coleridge's Theory of Imagination," *Studies in Romanticism*, 37 (1998), 259–277.

much they may include the dark side of our nature—are very far from heterodox. Harding's caveats are seen, though, as salutary reminders, for Reid goes on: "Within Coleridge's later thinking, then, I suggest that the *Biographia* definition is insufficiently qualified (is simply too grand) in its implicit claims for the human imagination, for it fails to acknowledge the ways in which our fallenness prevents any genuine repetition of the divine act in our own creativity—and Coleridge's own poems are redolent with a sense of an epiphany never quite actualized" (pp. 276–277).

But let me in turn qualify Reid's qualification of Harding. Surely, no one was more aware of our human "fallenness" than Coleridge, but Coleridge would never admit this fallenness is such as to prevent "any *genuine* repetition of the divine act in our own creativity," although he would admit that it prevents the *fullness* or *perfection* of that act. We are sorely limited by our fallen nature, to be sure, but Coleridge would insist that the creativity we have is both genuine and divinely given.

A recent study of Coleridge, though not focused primarily on either symbol or imagination, paints a broad and compelling picture of him which allows both imagination and symbol to be seen in new and fascinating ways. The book is Seamus Perry's *Coleridge and the Uses of Division* (1999),[18] a richly textured study of "the doubled theme of unity and division" in Coleridge (p. 1), whom Perry sees as "a man in two minds about which of two minds a man should be in" (p. 2), that is, "divided between the rival attractions of unity and division themselves" (p. 4). Coleridge's thought, he contends, "is best understood, not as the solution to a *problem*, but as the experience and exploration of a *muddle*" (p. 6)—a richly creative "muddle"—"muddle in its noblest aspect, a whole-hearted dealing with intractables" (p. 9).

What is at issue is no small muddle, but rather some of

---

[18] *Coleridge and the Uses of Division* (Oxford, 1999).

the most important tensions of Coleridge's life. For in Coleridge "there is at work a persistent opposition of intellectual and imaginative commitments, between the appeals of unity and the discernment of differences, between things considered as part of some whole and things regarded and enjoyed in their own right" (p. 23). In this broad context, both imagination and symbol can be seen as primary means of reconciling (to use the Coleridgean word) "the rival attractions of unity and division," of wholeheartedly "dealing with intractables."

Thus, Perry argues, "the Imagination promises rich and irreproachable bringings-together, which bestow a powerful affirmative magic not only on the unity it creates but also on the empirical particularity of the elements it takes up, so achieving at once the sensuous density of 'plenitude' and the unified totality of 'comprehensibility.' " For the imagination, Perry goes on, "has the hallmark Coleridgean quality of trying to have things both ways: it is a faculty devoted at once to unifying *and yet* to particularising" (p. 34). And symbol, the product of this faculty, "resonates with the fascination of the One and the Many"; for "something is symbolical when it retains its individuality while subsumed within (and symbolising) a greater whole—which, in Coleridge's own words, 'while it enunciates the whole, abides itself as a living part in the Unity, of which it is the representative' " (p. 88). This astute and admirably Coleridgean book—itself highly individual while enunciating a comprehensive and comprehensible whole—will undoubtedly resonate with Coleridge scholars for years to come.

Coleridge, whose mind never ceased to search and question, would surely approve this continuing tradition of scholarship and discovery.

1

Theological Foundations of Coleridge on Imagination

ONE BEGINS, invariably and perhaps inevitably, with Coleridge's definition of imagination at the end of the abortive Chapter XIII of the *Biographia Literaria*. "The primary IMAGINATION I hold to be the living Power and prime Agent of all human Perception, and as a repetition in the finite mind of the eternal act of creation in the infinite I AM. The secondary I consider as an echo of the former, co-existing with the conscious will, yet still as identical with the primary in the *kind* of its agency, and differing only in *degree*, and in the *mode* of its operation."[1]

What is clear, first of all, is that primary imagination belongs to us all, that Coleridge's description is, very typically, a description of our common human experience. Were it not for primary imagination, the world around us would be perceived as chaos: a mass of swirling atoms, a blur of colors, shapes, and sounds. There is a deep underlying unity among them, to be sure, for they all share, each in its own way, in the reality of God's being; but they are at the same time wildly different from one another, with a wildness that would appear to us chaotic were we not able to shape them into meaning. But, in fact, we instinctively—even the least orderly or artistic of us—order our experience, creating meaningful wholes: landscapes, groups, relationships of shapes, sounds, and colors. We are, all of us, shapers of our experience of what would otherwise appear a chaotic world around us. In the Coleridgean "system," this instinctive movement is founded upon an implicit act of faith. As Cath-

---

[1] *Biographia Literaria*, ed. Engell and Bate, I, 304. This will be cited hereafter as *BL*.

erine Miles Wallace writes of Coleridge's view, "any orderly explanation—any human act creating order—is grounded in an act of faith. This is not directly nor necessarily a faith in God but, rather, a faith in the possibility of order and knowledge that for many individuals has culminated in religious experience."[2] We believe instinctively in the possibility of order, and we act instinctively to order our perception of the world.

The artist, of course, does more. Secondary imagination allows the artist not only to perceive the world in an orderly way, but also to express that order in a new medium, be it paint or marble or, for the poet, words. The artist breaks down, "dissolves," the unity he or she has perceived in and among the natural shapes of trees and clouds and horses and human faces—a unity that is truly there by virtue of the participation of all these things in the world of being[3]—to allow a new chaos to emerge, as it were, and then to shape a new unity out of the artist's own consciousness of it, expressing it in watercolors or plaster or the sounds of music.

What is common to both these actions, however—that of all of us and that of the artist—is that each one is "a repetition in the finite mind of the eternal act of creation in the infinite I AM," the one an "echo" of the other. Can a human action truly be conceived of as the same kind of activity as the divine act of creation? Coleridge clearly believes so. For God, the "eternal act of creation" is the act by which God brings order or "cosmos" out of the "chaos" that existed before Creation. For us, primary imagination is the faculty by which we perceive the world as ordered, much as gestalt psychology has taught that we naturally shape our experience into meaningful patterns. Secondary imagination, whatever the difference in medium, does the same: shapes the chaos of experience into meaningful patterns. Both pri-

---

[2] *The Design of Biographia Literaria* (London, 1983), p. 11.
[3] On the philosophical notion of participation and the analogy of being, see J. Robert Barth, S.J., *Coleridge and Christian Doctrine* (Cambridge, Mass., 1969; repr. ed. New York, 1987), pp. 19–21.

mary and secondary imagination share in the "eternal act of creation" because they both have as their function to bring order out of chaos, as God did in the act of Creation. Thus, both the ordinary citizen and the artist share in the divine creative power, not indeed in the same degree, but nonetheless really.

Coleridge's definition assumes, too, a connaturality between the human mind and the divine mind. Or rather, it implies, even more than connaturality, an actual participation of the finite mind in the activity of the infinite mind, a "repetition in the finite mind of the eternal act of creation." God's "act of creation" is "eternal," and it is in this act that we—whether poet or ordinary citizen—participate here and now. Even as we exercise our creative faculties, God continues to constitute the world, including us, in being. Nor does one have to resort to a Berkeleian philosophy in order to affirm that God continues to constitute the world. The belief that God is continuously active in creation, keeping it in being by the abiding divine presence, is the ancient orthodoxy of all the Schoolmen: if God did not continue to be creatively present to all creation (the medieval Scholastic term for this active presence is *conservatio*), creation would simply cease to be. Present to all creation, God is present in a special way to the intelligent beings of creation in their free actions; by this presence, this *concursus divinus* (as the Scholastics called it), God's creative mind and will are united to ours.

Something like this is implicit, I believe, in Coleridge's conception of the relationship between the human being and God in the human creative act. Human creative acts are of their very nature united with the ongoing creative acts of God. Thus, the human person is truly a creator, both through the perception (primary imagination) by which we actively unite ourselves to the created world around us and through the higher degree of creation we exercise (secondary imagination) in expressing the unity of the world, aesthetically, in new shapes and creative forms.

But we must claim even more for Coleridge's view of

imagination, and it is here that its theological implications will begin to be most evident and important. For imagination, in Coleridge's view, is a cognitive faculty of a high order. One of his most exalted descriptions of imagination is in the remarkable Appendix C of *The Statesman's Manual*, written within the year following the publication of the *Biographia Literaria*. Writing there of the *"discursive* understanding, which forms for itself general notions and terms of classification," he affirms that its characteristic is "Clearness without Depth. It contemplates the unity of things in their *limits* only, and is consequently a knowledge of superficies without substance." Far beyond this, however, is "the completing power which unites clearness with depth, the plenitude of the sense with the comprehensibility of the understanding," that is, "the IMAGINATION, impregnated with which the understanding itself becomes intuitive, and a living power." The imagination derives its power from what Coleridge generally takes to be the highest human power, the reason (what he calls in *Aids to Reflection* the "Practical Reason")—"reason substantiated and vital . . . the breath of the power of God, and a pure influence from the glory of the Almighty."[4] The clear implication throughout is that the imagination is a cognitive faculty—although perhaps only indirectly so—deeper and more comprehensive than the mere understanding, working under the aegis of the reason, which is the highest human cognitive faculty, and which itself contains sense, understanding, and imagination, "even as the mind contains its thoughts, and is present in and through them all."[5]

Deeper and more comprehensive than the understanding, the imagination is, in fact, a faculty of the transcendent, capable of perceiving and in some degree articulating transcendent reality—the reality of higher realms of being, including the divine. In a remarkable essay in which he calls

---

[4] *Lay Sermons*, ed. R. J. White, vol. 6 of *The Collected Works*, ed. Coburn (Princeton, 1972), p. 69. This will be cited hereafter as *LS*.

[5] *LS*, pp. 69–70.

for "a new vision in theology," James S. Cutsinger argues cogently that in the "polarity" that underlies Coleridge's theory of imagination—indeed underlies most of his thought—"Coleridge is attempting to awaken nothing other than a possible way of seeing God."[6] In the context of imagination, this polarity is perhaps expressed nowhere more eloquently than in the other *locus classicus*, in Chapter XIV of the *Biographia Literaria*:

> The poet, described in *ideal* perfection, brings the whole soul of man into activity, with the subordination of its faculties to each other, according to their relative worth and dignity. He diffuses a tone, and spirit of unity, that blends, and (as it were) *fuses*, each into each, by that synthetic and magical power, to which we have exclusively appropriated the name of imagination. This power, first put in action by the will and understanding, and retained under their irremissive, though gentle and unnoticed, controul (*laxis effertur habenis*) reveals itself in the balance or reconciliation of opposite or discordant qualities: of sameness, with difference; of the general, with the concrete; the idea, with the image; the individual, with the representative; the sense of novelty and freshness, with old and familiar objects; a more than usual state of emotion, with more than usual order; judgment ever awake and steady self-possession, with enthusiasm and feeling profound or vehement; and while it blends and harmonizes the natural and the artificial, still subordinates art to nature; the manner to the matter; and our admiration of the poet to our sympathy with the poetry.[7]

It should be emphasized that Coleridgean polarity, whether applied to poetry or science or any other kind of knowledge, is not simply a tension between two essentially antagonistic forces; it is, rather, a fruitful sharing between two "forces" of one "power." As Coleridge wrote in one of his note-

---

[6] "Coleridgean Polarity and Theological Vision," *Harvard Theological Review*, 76 (1983), 92. One of the most perceptive treatments of Coleridge's idea of polarity is found in Owen Barfield's *What Coleridge Thought* (Middletown, Conn., 1971), chaps. 3 and 4.

[7] *BL*, II, 15–17.

books: "Polarity is not a Composite Force, or *vis tertia* constituted by the moments [movements?] of two counter-agents. It is 1 manifested in 2, not 1 + 1 = 2. . . . The polar forces are the two forms, in which a one [*sic*] Power works in the same act and instant. Thus, it is not the *Power*, Attraction and the Power Repulsion at once tugging and tugging like two sturdy Wrestlers that compose the Magnet; but The Magnetic Power working at once positively and negatively. Attraction and Repulsion are the two Forces of the one magnetic Power."[8] Although Coleridge frequently applies his theory of polarity to science as well as poetry, Cutsinger is after bigger game than either—as, of course, is Coleridge—and so turns his discussion of polarity to what he calls "the chief problem facing today's theologian: the problem of the knowledge of God."[9]

The problem of knowledge in any realm, Cutsinger makes clear, is "a problem of barriers or dividing surfaces."[10] In much of modern theology, he finds, an "oppressive set of dividing surfaces" has arisen between the world and God. "Skepticism has made it appear . . . that ours is a world of us and them: that there is, on the one hand, a region continuous with the self or subject, flowing under the direction of its own power and activity; and, on the other hand, a second region, discontinuous with the self or subject, possessing unknown and unknowable motions and configurations of its own." The result in theology has been a series of dichotomies between "the immanent and the transcendent, reason and revelation, the secular and the sacred, the scientific and the religious, and the natural and the supernatural."[11] It is precisely here, Cutsinger believes, that the Coleridgean polarity can help. If the task of the theologian is to "render intelligible man's relationship to a God who is forever overflowing custom's bounds," the theologian must

---

[8] Egerton ms. 2801, f. 128; quoted by Barfield in *What Coleridge Thought*, p. 203, n. 24.
[9] Cutsinger, p. 101.
[10] Cutsinger, p. 101.
[11] Cutsinger, p. 102.

do so in a vision that is true both to the divine reality and to the human experience of that reality, to allow "for the immanence *yet* transcendence, the sameness *yet* otherness, the 'in' of the 'out,' and the 'out' of the 'in' of this strange one called God."[12] Hence, what Coleridge offers is not merely a new language, but a mode of "transforming vision." The exercise of imagination, which can (as Coleridge writes in the *Biographia Literaria*) "awaken the mind's attention from the lethargy of custom," can open our eyes to "the loveliness and the wonders of the world before us,"[13] thereby revealing (in Cutsinger's fine phrase) "a world translucent to deity."[14]

Coleridge's theory of imagination, grounded in Coleridgean polarity, is deeply bound up with his vital philosophy. The merely "mechanical" mind can see only oppositions or, at best, the juxtaposition of separate realities. The mind, however, that is imbued with a "living and spiritual philosophy" can envision two distinct realities— two "counter-powers"—actually "interpenetrating" each other, so that each shares in the being of the other.[15] Such

---

[12] Cutsinger, p. 105.

[13] *BL*, II, 7.

[14] Cutsinger, p. 93. Since imagination not only has to do with knowledge and vision but also involves the activity of the will (imagination, "first put in action by the will and understanding," brings "the whole soul of man into activity"), perhaps the Coleridgean idea of imagination can also help in articulating the ancient theological problem of the relationship between divine action and human action, especially between the eternal foreknowledge implicit in the doctrine of divine providence and the freedom affirmed for itself by the human spirit. This was the problem the medieval theory of *concursus divinus* (mentioned earlier) was designed to solve. If, as Coleridge insists, the divine and human powers truly "interpenetrate"—if they are indeed "two forces of one power"— then the paradox of divine foreknowledge and human freedom may be perceived as considerably less vexing. Perhaps there can be a divine "leading of the Spirit" without loss of what we perceive as our freedom to choose, since the divine knowledge and the human action would be two "forces" of a single "power," which has its origin in God—the human action being "a repetition in the finite mind of the eternal act of creation in the infinite I AM." In terms of Coleridge's "interpenetration," such a free human act could be seen as at the same time truly divine and truly human—in theological terms, both graced and free.

[15] *LS*, p. 89.

a "living" vision, and only such a vision, can encompass immanent and transcendent, human and divine, the reality of the self and the reality of God, in a single act of knowing. It is no accident that the *Biographia Literaria* ends with a paean of praise to the Logos, the pattern of Creation, through whom—as the incarnate Christ—mankind and God most fully "interpenetrate."

However, such a vision as we have described requires a language commensurate with its complexity; we find just such a language in Coleridge's language of symbol. "An IDEA," he writes, "in the *highest* sense of that word"—and by this he means the supersensuous knowledge involved in religion, philosophy, and art—"cannot be conveyed but by a *symbol*; and, except in geometry, all symbols of necessity involve an apparent contradiction."[16] It is for this reason that "a great idea can be taught gradually, that is by considering it as a germ which cannot appear at any one moment in all of its force."[17] On this latter text, Catherine Miles Wallace very aptly remarks: "In most fields, the 'great idea' *must* be taught gradually if it is to emerge from a discursive text." This is because, she goes on, except in geometry, "symbols communicate ideas more adequately than discursive logical formulations, because a symbol holds together the contradictions that logic can only break apart."[18] And these contradictions—or at least seeming contradictions—include the material and the spiritual, the human and the divine, the temporal and the eternal. A symbol, Coleridge writes, "is characterized . . . above all by the translucence of the Eternal through and in the Temporal. It always partakes of the Reality which it renders intelligible; and while it enunciates the whole, abides itself as a living part in that Unity, of which it is the representative."[19] Symbol, therefore, not merely expresses the juxtaposition of two realities

---

[16] *BL*, I, 156.
[17] *The Philosophical Lectures of Samuel Taylor Coleridge*, ed. Kathleen Coburn (New York, 1949), p. 173.
[18] Wallace, pp. 9–10.
[19] *LS*, p. 30.

(as metaphor can do) but also articulates, however dimly, the "interpenetration" of two disparate and often seemingly very distant realities, such as humankind and God. It is by such language—poetic language—that the chasm between the immanent and the transcendent can be bridged.

Philosopher and theologian Bernard Lonergan parallels Coleridge's thought when he points to a passage through several modes of discourse in the transmission of divine revelation.[20] The first is the scriptural or interpersonal mode, in which the personal experience of religion is expressed in literary form: narratives, parables, personal discourses, sermons, hymns, prayers—the sorts of forms that make up the Old and New Testaments. In time, the desire for deeper understanding moves the tradition in the direction of a theological mode of discourse—more philosophical, more systematic—as thinkers strive to probe the meaning of revelation. This style sacrifices the intimacy and symbolic appeal of scripture for the clarity of theological discourse. The theological mode in turn gives way to a conciliar or dogmatic mode of discourse, the more apodictic, authoritative style that characterizes the Councils of the Church; here the findings of theologians may be confirmed or defined. Then there may be a return to the theological mode, as theologians explore the meaning of doctrine and the relationship of doctrines to one another. But theology and doctrine must be returned at last to the interpersonal, scriptural mode—both to further understand them and to preach them—because it is in this essentially literary, symbolic mode of discourse that the mystery of the revelation is most fully respected. What it sacrifices in clarity, it more than makes up for in the richness of its complexity. It is in this symbolic expression that the human spirit can most fully and deeply encounter the personal reality of God; in other words, it is in such a symbolic encounter that one can experience Coleridge's "translucence of the Eternal through and in the Temporal."

---

[20] *Divinarum Personarum Conceptio Analogica* (Rome, 1957), pp. 7–51, esp. pp. 31–32.

John Coulson is on very much the same path when he speaks of Coleridge's "fiduciary use of language,"[21] arguing persuasively that Coleridge's use of and reflection on language returns to the tradition of seventeenth-century divines like Donne and Hooker, who believed that "language is for action as well as reflection," that language is meant to evoke a response of the whole person.[22] Such language is essentially symbolic, because it maintains the complexity of reality, allowing even contradictory aspects of experience to be expressed in the same utterance. As Coulson expresses it, the poet (in the Coleridgean conception) "confronts us with a use of language in which words do not stand for terms possessing a constant meaning but are to be seen as components in a field of force that take their value from the charge of the field as a *whole*."[23] Lecturing on Shakespeare, Coleridge sees the imagination, "as it were, hovering between images. As soon as it is fixed on one image, it becomes understanding; but while it is unfixed and wavering between them, attaching itself permanently to none, it is imagination."[24] This is a kind of language, and perhaps a

---

[21] *Newman and the Common Tradition: A Study in the Language of Church and Society* (Oxford, 1970), pp. 3–13. Another remarkable book that probes sensitively the nature of religious language, especially in the nineteenth century, is Stephen Prickett's *Words and the Word: Language, Poetics and Biblical Interpretation* (Cambridge, 1986). Prickett is particularly cogent and helpful in his consideration (pp. 105–123) of the important eighteenth-century theologian and Orientalist Robert Lowth, whose *Lectures on the Sacred Poetry of the Hebrews* Prickett calls "the book that was to transform biblical studies in England and Germany alike, and which was to do more than any other single work to make the biblical tradition, rather than the neo-classical one, the central poetic tradition of the Romantics" (p. 105). Prickett is also excellent in his discussion of religious language in Wordsworth (especially in *The Prelude*, pp. 96–104), Coleridge (pp. 134–148 and passim), Newman (especially pp. 66–68 and 217–220), and Hopkins (especially pp. 118–123).

[22] Coulson, p. 13.

[23] Coulson, p. 10.

[24] *Shakespearean Criticism*, ed. T. M. Raysor (London, 1960), II, 103. In R. A. Foakes's more recent edition, the passage reads somewhat less eloquently. Coleridge describes the imagination "when it is hovering between two images: as soon as it is fixed <on one> it becomes understanding; and when it is waving between them attaching itself to neither it is

kind of analysis, that theologians today might find uniquely valuable. To return to Coulson: "This is a failure of language in one respect—to pin the words down to exact and determinate meanings—but it is also a success—the diverse and apparently contradictory aspects of a complex experience are being held in the unity which is its essential character, and in terms of which it can alone be adequately communicated to us."[25]

In short, one can claim, in Coleridgean terms, that it is only imagination that can bring us to the full encounter with religious reality, because it is only symbolic language that resists the human drive for clarity and determinateness. The divine, the numinous, the transcendent, can never be encompassed by the clarity of "consequent Reasoning." It can only be intimated, guessed at, caught out of the corner of the eye; and for this, only the ambiguity of symbolic utterance will serve. Catherine Miles Wallace rightly insists that for Coleridge "a closed logical system excludes the divine."[26] As he wrote in an annotation to *The Friend*, "the inevitable result of all consequent Reasoning, in which the intellect refuses to acknowledge a higher or deeper ground than it can itself supply . . . ever has been—PANTHEISM under one or other of its modes."[27] Symbolic language, on the other hand, is not closed but open—open to the possibilities, the hints and guesses, the intimations, even the momentary glimpses, of divine reality.

But if symbolic language—what Coulson calls Coleridge's "fiduciary language"—is open to the intimations of the divine, we have suggested that it is also open in another important way: it is open to the response, not only intellectual but emotive, of the human listener to such language.

---

imagination"; *Lectures 1808–1819 On Literature*, ed. R. A. Foakes, vol. 5 of *The Collected Works*, ed. Coburn, 2 vols. (Princeton, 1987), I, 311. Foakes's edition will be cited hereafter as *LL*.

[25] Coulson, p. 11.

[26] Wallace, p. 10.

[27] *The Friend*, ed. Barbara E. Rooke, vol. 4 of *The Collected Works*, ed. Coburn, 2 vols. (Princeton, 1969), I, 523, note. This will be cited hereafter as *FR*.

Symbol involves for Coleridge an act of faith, calling for a response of the whole person, indeed a commitment of one's self. In Coleridgean terms, symbolic experience not only involves a new awareness of divine reality, but is, at least potentially, an encounter with the transcendent reality of God and a call to engage oneself in the process of discovering and meeting God even more deeply.

This is indeed, we should add, a question of process. In addition to allowing for the preservation and articulation of complexity, symbol also allows for growth: growth in the perceiver as well as in the reality perceived, or, perhaps better, growth in the cognitive union between them. Since symbolic language remains an expression of mystery, it is (in I. A. Richards's telling phrase) "inexhaustible to meditation."[28] By such meditation, one comes at the same time to a deeper knowledge of the other that is the object of meditation and, because of the "interpenetration" of subject and object, to new knowledge of the mysteries of one's self. We come to know ourselves in knowing what is not ourselves.

This "process" is, of course, profoundly Coleridgean. In most of his published work, Coleridge's aim is precisely to engage his reader in the activity of thought. One need only think of *The Friend*, the *Lay Sermons*, and *Aids to Reflection* to realize how true this is. Coleridge's remark in an early essay of *The Friend* is typical: "Where then a subject, that demands thought, has been thoughtfully treated, and with an exact and patient derivation from its principles, we must be willing to exert a portion of the same effort, and to *think* with the author, or the author will have thought in vain for us."[29] Thought for Coleridge involves quest and discovery, and he expects his readers to join him on the quest, with Coleridge as his intellectual friend and guide. To return to Lonergan's paradigm for a moment: Coleridge constantly forces language in the direction of the interpersonal mode of discourse. Hence, his constant use, even in the most

---

[28] *Coleridge on Imagination* (Bloomington, Ind., 1960), p. 171.
[29] *FR*, I, 25.

seemingly abstruse arguments, of concrete and telling metaphors. He will use the conciliar and theological modes, especially in his private notebooks, but in public discourse his
primary goal is to *encounter* his readers, to engage them
actively in the excitement of his own quest and its discov-
eries.

In addition to all the other characteristics of the Coleridgean imagination we have suggested, there is one that, in
a sense, overarches all the others: its power to unify the
various kinds of human knowledge. For imagination is not
merely a faculty of poetic and religious knowledge—on
which we have been particularly focusing—but also, as
Coleridge says in the *Biographia Literaria*, the "prime
agent of all human perception." Thus, for Coleridge all
human knowledge—sense perception, scientific insight,
aesthetic experience, philosophical reflection, theological
meditation, and whatever other ways the human mind can
know—involves the exercise of imagination, the faculty by
which the multiform reality of the world is seen in relationship. As theologians and literary critics and theorists today
strive to relate the results of their work to the work of scholars in other disciplines—whether it be the laboratory research of geneticists, the semiotic theories of post-
structuralists, or the critical analyses of film critics—
perhaps the study of imagination as Coleridge conceived it
might be a means of achieving mutual understanding of
what is common to disciplines seemingly far distant from
one another. Perhaps for us, as for Coleridge, knowledge
can once more come to be seen as one, and all reflective—as
Coleridge also believed—of the one eternal Logos, the supreme symbol, the primal sacrament.

2

Symbol as Sacrament

HAVING ARGUED for a theological foundation for Coleridge's theory of imagination, we now turn more specifically to his view of symbol, the product of the imaginative act. In a sense we are turning our focus from the faculty to its utterance, from the poet to the poem, and from a theology to a sacrament that touches lives and hearts.

Considering how relatively little Coleridge wrote expressly on symbol, it is remarkable how central it is in his thinking. He often said, in fact, that one of his primary aims was to teach English thinkers—whether fundamentalists on the right or rationalists on the left—that there is a middle ground between the literal and the metaphorical. Especially in his later thought—during the years, say, from 1815 to 1834—symbol seems so often to be present. Whether he is talking of idea, of method, of faith, or of poetry, even when he does not use the word "symbol," the concept always seems to be there, lurking on the "periphery of advertence." Yet few critics have attempted to come to grips with it, at least insofar as we find it outside the context of poetry itself. But it is precisely outside the context of poetry and poetic theory that I think we must look to learn the deepest meaning of Coleridge's idea of symbol.

The *locus classicus*, in *The Statesman's Manual*—a passage we have touched on already—remains the best place to begin. Here, in his discussion of Scripture and the nature of scriptural truth, Coleridge makes much of the distinction between allegory (or metaphor) and symbol:

> It is among the miseries of the present age that it recognizes no medium between *Literal* and *Metaphorical*. Faith is either to be buried in the dead letter, or its name and honors usurped

by a counterfeit product of the mechanical understanding, which in the blindness of self-complacency confounds Symbols with Allegories. Now an Allegory is but a translation of abstract notions into a picture-language which is itself nothing but an abstraction from objects of the senses; the principal being more worthless even than its phantom proxy, both alike unsubstantial, and the former shapeless to boot. On the other hand a Symbol . . . is characterized by a translucence of the Special in the Individual or of the General in the Especial or of the Universal in the General. Above all by the translucence of the Eternal through and in the Temporal. It always partakes of the Reality which it renders intelligible; and while it enunciates the whole, abides itself as a living part in that Unity, of which it is the representative.[1]

What, then, is the crucial point of difference between the allegorical or the merely metaphorical, and the symbolic? Clearly, as has been so often pointed out, a symbol "always partakes of the Reality which it renders intelligible." We see this too, much earlier, in the long letter of September 10, 1802, to William Sotheby. The word "symbol" does not appear, but the concept is clearly in Coleridge's mind. "Nature has her proper interest; & he will know what it is, who believes & feels, that every Thing has a Life of it's own, & that we are all *one Life*. A Poet's *Heart & Intellect* should be *combined*, intimately combined & *unified*, with the great appearances in Nature—& not merely held in solution & loose mixture with them, in the shape of formal Similies [*sic*]."[2] The "one Life within us and abroad" of

---

[1] *LS*, p. 30.

[2] *Collected Letters of Samuel Taylor Coleridge*, ed. Earl Leslie Griggs, 6 vols. (Oxford, 1956–1971), II, 864. This will be cited hereafter as *CL*. See also Appendix C of *The Statesman's Manual*: "By a symbol I mean, not a metaphor or allegory or any other figure of speech or form of fancy, but an actual and essential part of that, the whole of which it represents" (*LS*, p. 79). There is also an interesting discussion of allegory and symbol in the as yet unpublished holograph notebook—known as the "clasped vellum" notebook—that Coleridge kept from 1814 to 1825. This notebook, now in the Berg Collection of the New York Public Library, is actually Notebook 29 of the numbered series of Coleridge's notebooks, most of which are in the British Museum. I quote two brief passages from it, with the kind permission of the Curator of the Berg Collection.

"The Eolian Harp" is distant only in time from the reflection, twenty years later, in *The Statesman's Manual*.

All this has been said often enough: a symbol, for Coleridge, always partakes of the reality it represents. But there remains a further question, not so often asked: what is it that allows this to be so? What is there in his view of reality that allows him to see "one Life within us and abroad," to assert implicitly that a given reality, whether material or spiritual, is essentially linked with all other reality—that we live in a world of symbols and, therefore, of symbolic knowledge? The answer lies in what we may call his principle of the "consubstantiality" of all being, clearly akin to the traditional notion of the analogy of all being. For the term "consubstantial" we need turn back only one page from the quotation we have already seen from *The Statesman's Manual*. Speaking of the scriptures, Coleridge describes the faculty of imagination as "that reconciling and mediatory power, which incorporating the Reason in Images of the Sense, and organizing (as it were) the flux of the Senses by the permanence and self-circling energies of the Reason, gives birth to a system of symbols, harmonious in themselves, and consubstantial with the truths, of which they are the *conductors*."[3] Nor is it only the products of the

---

"A connected Series of Metaphors to one Whole is an Allegory.—And where the Metaphors adopted conventionally by all classes of a society, so that the objects, to which the assimilation is implied, are Symbols or partake of the Nature of Symbols, and are assumed as already known & understood by the Auditor,—this Allegory, so qualified, is *A Fable*; & this alone merits the name of an Esopic [*sic*] Fable.—The Ass, the Fox, the Lion, the Oak, the Wolf, the Lamb are all either συμβολα or ως συμβολα . . ." Notebook 29, f. 59.

"It will often happen, that in the extension of human knowledge what had been an *Allegory*, will become a *Symbol*. Thus: the identification, in genere, of the vegetable Life with the animal life, as the same power in a lower dignity, would raise the Homeric Allegory or compound Metaphor ['the lives of men are like the leaves . . .'?—JRB] into a Symbol." Notebook 29, f. 61.

For an excellent history of the development of the Romantic distinction between allegory and symbol—beginning with Goethe, Schelling, and A. W. Schlegel—see Tzvetan Todorov's *Theories of the Symbol*, pp. 198–221.

[3] *LS*, p. 29.

human imagination, the poetry of the scriptures, that are to be read as symbolic. The same is true of "another book, likewise a revelation of God—the great book of his servant Nature." For "it is the *poetry* of all human nature, to read it likewise in a figurative sense, and to find therein correspondencies [*sic*] and symbols of the spiritual world."[4]

What is included in this symbolic perception of reality? Potentially, as we have seen, it is unlimited in its scope: particular and universal, idea and image, new and old, subjective and objective. The imagination, which is always for Coleridge the symbol-making faculty, is the unifying faculty, and what it can unify is as broad as all reality. Add to this description of the symbolic imagination (and so implicitly of the symbol itself) the description we have already seen—"a Symbol . . . is characterized by a translucence of the Special in the Individual or of the General in the Especial or of the Universal in the General. Above all by the translucence of the Eternal through and in the Temporal"— and it is clear that symbol potentially encompasses the depth of humanity itself and the height and breadth of all the world, in and out of time. Symbolic knowledge reaches out to all the human mind can know.

With this in mind, we might do well to avoid the kind of distinction made, for example, by James Volant Baker in his otherwise excellent treatment of Coleridge on symbol. Baker distinguishes quite sharply between Romantic symbol and modern symbol: "The romantic was vertical, if we assume the old scheme of the chain of being; something 'below,' on the physical plane, was the analogy of something 'above' on the plane of ideas or spiritual realities. In modern symbolism, 'above' and 'below' have been abolished, and modern symbolism is horizontal, the symbol chosen being a means of conveying the author's manifold experience of life as we know it."[5] The implication of

---

[4] *LS*, Appendix C, p. 70.
[5] *The Sacred River: Coleridge's Theory of the Imagination* (Baton Rouge, La., 1957), pp. 210–211.

Baker's distinction is that Coleridge's notion of symbol does not properly apply to "modern" symbolists (his examples are Kafka and Mann, Eliot and Yeats), but only to the poets of an earlier age. But in the face of Coleridge's rich idea of symbol—as well as in the face of the practice of the best symbol-makers in any age, like Dante, Shakespeare, Wordsworth, as well as Kafka and Mann, Eliot and Yeats—such a distinction seems an unjustified narrowing of the scope of symbol. Baker seems to be content with an analysis of modern literature that "flattens out" the actuality of symbol, that sees modern poetry lacking the transcendent element of symbol so important in Coleridge, leaving a wholly "secular" form of symbol in its place. But in the very best of artists, including the ones he adduces, symbol reaches both vertically and horizontally, as it does for Coleridge.

Baker's distinction is similar to the distinction of Erich Kahler between descending and ascending symbolism. Descending symbolism is "all symbolism in which symbolic representation detaches itself, descends to us, from a prior and higher reality, a reality determining, and therefore superior to, its symbolic meaning. That is to say, genuinely mythical and cultic works are not intended as symbolic representation, they are meant to describe real happenings. It is we who, a posteriori, derive a symbolic meaning from them."[6] Ascending symbolism, on the other hand, is "a new creation entirely, springing from artistic imagination. Here, no external, pre-existent material is furnished to the artist; no longer is he guided by cultic patterns. He is free to create images which, though being unique, singular forms, imply something commonly human. In such works the symbol reaches the stage of consummate representation."[7] Coleridge would find this distinction, I think, as unnecessary or as unjustified as Baker's. The product of the symbol-making faculty is never "a new creation entirely." It is always a

---

[6] "The Nature of the Symbol," in *Symbolism in Religion and Literature*, ed. Rollo May (New York, 1960), p. 65.

[7] Kahler, p. 67.

reconciliation of the old and the new, the temporal and the eternal, the immanent and the transcendent, the objective and the subjective. The maker or perceiver is always part of the symbol, just as is, potentially, every dimension of external reality. There are differences in emphasis from age to age and from person to person, but symbol itself remains always open-ended; one leg always, in John Unterecker's phrase, "kicks at the stars."[8] Since all reality is "consubstantial," all reality is capable of symbolic representation.

Coleridge's idea of consubstantiality is very much like the traditional philosophical conception of the "participation" of all being, which is the basis of the Renaissance "great chain of being." All beings, from God down to the lowest finite forms, share in "being." With this, the way is open for common predication among all things—analogously but really. A molecule is beautiful, a stone is beautiful, an animal is beautiful, a man is beautiful, God is beautiful. They are not all beautiful in the same way, but they all can legitimately be called beautiful, and this naming somehow corresponds to reality. One might say, with Robert Burns, "O My Luve's like a red, red rose." Or one might say, with St. Paul, that the marriage of a man and a woman is symbolic of the covenant between Christ and his people. In each case, the attribution is no mere fiction; there is a shared reality, analogous (different, yet in some way the same) but real. In learning something about the beauty of a rose, one learns something new about the beauty of the beloved; in learning something about the love of a man and a woman, one learns something new about the meaning of the scriptural phrase "God is love." Beauty is somehow one, love is somehow one, being is somehow one. "Turn but a stone and start a wing."

This predication is not possible, obviously, of all characteristics; most of the examples adduced above are based on the so-called "transcendental properties" of being, which are attributable to all beings without exception. Other quali-

---

[8] *A Reader's Guide to William Butler Yeats* (New York, 1959), p. 34.

ties are attributable to some beings, not to others. We can say, for example, that a plant, an animal, a man, and God, all share analogously (each in its own way) the characteristic of life; we cannot say this of a stone. But once we admit the universal transcendence of being itself and of the transcendental properties of being (commonly taken to be one, true, good, and beautiful), the way is open for the more limited but still wide-ranging sharing of reality on many levels. Something like this, I believe, is what Coleridge means by the consubstantiality of the symbol.

But there remains the problem of perception. On what does Coleridge base such a view? How does one perceive this consubstantiality, this oneness of all things that makes symbolism possible? There seems to be implicit a kind of act of faith in this oneness. Exactly so. Symbol-making— and indeed symbol-perceiving—is for Coleridge essentially a religious act. In order to understand his idea of symbol, we must ultimately place the discussion in a religious context, where alone we can find its true meaning.

Nor should this be surprising, if we take into account the extraordinary "wholeness" of Coleridge's thinking. For him, all knowledge is ultimately one, whether it be scientific, poetic, philosophical, or religious, and the capstone of all knowledge for him is knowledge of God. We might also have found a hint in the word "consubstantial" itself as it is applied to symbol. Its origins are perfectly clear; it is the privileged word canonized by the Council of Nicaea in A.D. 325 to express the relationship of the Son to the Father in the Trinity. Coleridge once referred to it (in its Greek form) as "the dear lucky *homoousios*, that had set all Christendom by the ears"![9] It is somehow fitting that Coleridge's prime analogate for this word should be an expression of the deepest and highest unity possible (the unity of the Godhead), together with the most meaningful and closest relationship

---

[9] Notebook 35 (c. 1827), f. 43. The quotation from this still unpublished notebook is used with the kind permission of the late Mr. A. H. B. Coleridge, great-great-grandson of the poet.

of difference (the Persons of the Trinity). For this unity and difference, within the framework of deeply shared reality (it "partakes of the Reality which it renders intelligible"), are of the essence of symbol for Coleridge. The Son truly "symbolizes" the Father; he "images him forth," at the same time partaking in the most perfect possible way in the inner reality of the Father.

But the more obvious source is the one with which we began chapter 1, the definition of the imagination, the symbol-making and symbol-perceiving faculty in Chapter XIII of the *Biographia Literaria*: "The Primary IMAGINATION I hold to be the living Power and Prime Agent of all human Perception, and as a repetition in the finite mind of the eternal act of creation in the infinite I AM. The secondary I consider as an echo of the former, co-existing with the conscious will, yet still as identical with the primary in the *kind* of its agency, and differing only in *degree*, and in the *mode* of its operation."[10] We have seen that the act of perceiving symbols (primary imagination) or of making symbols (secondary imagination) is essentially a religious act, a finite participation in the infinite creative act of the supreme symbol-maker, the supreme symbol-perceiver, just as creation itself is (apart from the eternal processions of the Son from the Father and of the Spirit from the Father and Son) the supreme symbol. And what kind of religious act is it? At bottom, we have argued, it is an act of faith. As with the supreme symbol, creation, so with all other real symbols

---

[10] *BL*, I, 304. Sara Coleridge, the poet's daughter, notes about this passage: "This last clause 'and as a repetition,' &c. I find stroked out in a copy of the B.L. containing a few MS. marginal notes of the author. . . . I think it best to preserve the sentence, while I mention the author's judgment upon it, especially as it has been quoted." *Biographia Literaria*, ed. Henry Nelson Coleridge, 2 vols. (completed by Sara Coleridge), in *The Complete Works of Samuel Taylor Coleridge*, ed. W. G. T. Shedd, 7 vols. (New York, 1856), III, 363, note. In his note on this passage in his text of the *Biographia*, John Shawcross adds: "Probably Coleridge felt that the ideas which the sentence suggested were incongruous with the rest of the passage." *Biographia Literaria*, ed. John Shawcross, 2 vols. (Oxford, 1907), I, 272. Not finding this incongruity, I leave the passage as Coleridge originally wrote it.

(those which truly "partake of the Reality which they render intelligible"), an act of faith is necessary to perceive the true unity of being—the consubstantiality—within the differences. This is because the making or perceiving of a symbol, in Coleridge's view, always involves a union of subject and object. If there is to be a union of a thinking and willing subject with someone or something outside itself, there must be a commitment of self—involving trust and love as well as knowledge—an act of faith.

An act of faith, for Coleridge, is precisely that—a commitment of self. In his many writings, published and unpublished, on the problem of faith, he walked a careful line between the traditional Roman Catholic emphasis on faith as an act of knowing, essentially an intellectual act, and the Protestant emphasis on faith as an act of the will.[11] For him faith was a commitment of one's whole self, an act of intellect and will and emotions. Faith is not apart from hope and love, the other theological virtues; each one, if complete, includes the others. An act of faith is an act of love, a commitment of one's self to another. An act of faith, like the act of the poet, "brings the whole soul of man into activity."

In this sense, as in other ways as well, true symbol for Coleridge might be said to be "sacramental." Some of the similarities between sacrament and symbol will be strikingly obvious. A sacrament is a sensible sign—a spoken word of forgiveness, a ritual gesture, a material object (a piece of bread, a cup of wine)—pointing to something beyond itself. So, for Coleridge, is a symbol. A sacrament is an efficacious sign; it actually makes present what it represents—the grace of God, which is a share in the life of God. It "partakes of the Reality which it renders intelligible." So does a symbol. A sacrament—Baptism, Confirmation, Marriage, the Eucharist—involves the union of a subject and an object, the faithful recipient and the material sign in which the grace of God is mediated to the Christian. So

---

[11] On Coleridge's view of faith, see Barth, *Coleridge and Christian Doctrine*, chap. 2, esp. pp. 31–33.

does a symbol. A sacrament is one of the ways in which God shares divine power with the human family, allows them to act in God's name and with God's power; it is a finite participation in the infinite creative act of the I AM. So, for Coleridge, is a symbol.

But there is another aspect of sacrament that perhaps underscores even more than these its resemblance to Coleridge's view of symbol. It is a dimension of sacrament that has come to the fore again only recently in the work of theologians who have written on the nature of sacraments. It is a dimension that, I think, may be said to be one of Coleridge's special contributions to our thinking about symbol. It is the notion of sacrament—and symbol—as encounter.

The Dutch theologian Edouard Schillebeeckx contends that there has been a tendency during the past two centuries of theology toward "a purely impersonal, almost mechanical approach" to the sacraments, because they were considered "chiefly in terms of physical categories."[12] The response of much recent theology has been to found the study of sacraments on the concept of "human, personal encounter" (p. 3). Sacraments are ultimately "the properly human mode of encounter with God" (p. 6).

We are brought back at this point to our earlier suggestion that the making or perceiving of a symbol is for Coleridge a kind of act of faith. It is meant to evoke a response of the whole person, in faith, hope, and love. It is a commitment of self to someone other than oneself. What I am suggesting here is that this commitment is much like the commitment involved in the reception of a sacrament, particularly as Schillebeeckx conceives it: an encounter, through sensible reality, with God. Whether in or out of poetry, Coleridge's whole life was a quest for unity. For him the making and perceiving of symbols, particularly in poetry, is a kind of religious act, by which he encounters God, the ultimate reality and the source of all unity. The symbols of poetry and

---

[12] *Christ the Sacrament of the Encounter with God* (New York, 1963), p. 3.

art and the symbols of the material world are never allowed
to remain an end in themselves. Because there is a "consubstantiality" of all reality, all things—and all things that
stand as symbols of other things—say something of God,
the I AM. Only in this way can Coleridge resist the constant
temptation he sees in human beings to "break and scatter
the one divine and invisible life of nature into countless
idols of the sense."[13] For *the solution of Phaenomena can
never be derived from Phaenomena.*[14] But if symbols ultimately "partake of the Reality which they render intelligible"—God—then the only acceptable response to them is a
commitment of one's whole self, bringing "the whole soul
of man into activity." It is a response to sacrament in an act
of faith, and therefore an encounter of the human person
with God.

There is at work here what in scholastic philosophy is
called "mutual causality." The perception or the creation of
a symbol, in the sense in which I have described it, depends
wholly on the acceptance of the consubstantiality (in Coleridge's sense) of all things, especially the consubstantiality
of God and creation. Only if one accepts, by a kind of act
of faith, this consubstantiality, can one create or even perceive a sign that truly partakes of the reality it represents.
The commitment of self in faith in this way (and for Coleridge this is a commitment of the whole soul, in love as well
as in faith) is necessary for the perception of the symbol *as
symbol*, for the creation of symbol *as symbol*. At the same
time, the reverse is true; perception of the symbol is necessary in order for one to make such a commitment of faith
and love; one can commit oneself only to what one somehow already knows.

I have come at this notion somewhat by way of Paul Tillich, who speaks in his *Dynamics of Faith* of the "opening
up of reality" that takes place in symbol: "All arts create
symbols for a level of reality which cannot be reached in

---

[13] *FR*, I, 518.
[14] *FR*, I, 500. Italics in original. See also I, 500–524.

any other way."[15] It is very much as Coleridge would have it: "An IDEA, in the *highest* sense of that word, cannot be conveyed but by a *symbol*. . . ."[16] Tillich goes on to insist that the symbol

> not only opens up dimensions and elements of reality which otherwise would remain unapproachable but also unlocks dimensions and elements of our soul which correspond to the dimensions and elements of reality. A great play gives us not only a new vision of the human scene, but it opens up hidden depths of our own being. Thus we are able to receive what the play reveals to us in reality. There are within us dimensions of which we cannot become aware except through symbols, as melodies and rhythms in music.[17]

What the symbol does, then, for Tillich as for Coleridge, is to mediate between a subject and reality other than the self. It "reveals itself in the balance or reconciliation of opposite or discordant qualities,"[18] which are, however, not really opposite or discordant. They are different yet the same— analogous, ultimately consubstantial. There is not merely the "reconciliation" of the differences—general and concrete, idea and image, individual and representative (as in the *Biographia*); there is also a "translucence" of one to the other—"a translucence of the Special in the Individual or of the General in the Especial or of the Universal in the General. Above all by the translucence of the Eternal through and in the Temporal" (as in *The Statesman's Manual*).[19] It is through the mediation of symbol that growth takes place in the subject, the perceiver or creator of the symbol. We are opened up to reality, and reality is opened up to us. There is a kind of mutual dependence: we depend upon symbol, while symbol depends upon our creation or perception. We believe in the symbol as symbolic and find

---

[15] *Dynamics of Faith*, World Perspectives 10 (New York, 1956), p. 42.
[16] *BL*, I, 156.
[17] Tillich, pp. 42–43.
[18] *BL*, II, 16.
[19] *LS*, p. 30.

ourselves enriched by it. Thus enriched, we are able to commit ourselves more fully to the symbolic reality, and are able to perceive it more fully. Through this new perception, we are again enriched.

In *Newman and the Common Tradition*, John Coulson outlines much the same view in terms of Coleridge's notion of the Church as a symbol, underscoring both the aspect of growth and the aspect of the mutual dependence of symbol and perceiver. It is worth quoting at length:

> The conception of the Church which derives from Coleridge—that of symbol or idea—is of an 'organismus' which requires from us a similar organic and unified response: its function is to bring all the aspects of religion, all aspects of the believer into a unifying focus. We can understand this conception more exactly if we see how Coleridge talks of the sacrament of marriage: 'it is an outward sign co-essential with that which it signifies': it is a part of the whole in the sense of being an intensification of what we already experience, and not something different or separate. 'Thus the husband and wife exercise the duties of their marriage contract of love . . . all the year long, and yet solemnize it by a more deliberate and reflecting act of the same love on the anniversary of their marriage.'[20]

Our perception of the symbol is never complete, Coulson continues, because we ourselves are never complete:

> For Coleridge, sacrament and symbol are the particular forms for the realizing of religious assent. When we marry, are baptized, or go to Communion, we are performing the act necessary for the further and more complete understanding of our assent. We might say that the sacrament or symbol was the model for a performative utterance which, on performance, discloses a more complete understanding of the model—the model (or symbol) and our understanding of it being, therefore, 'the same thing but in different periods of its growth.'

---

[20] Coulson, p. 35. The sentences quoted are from *Aids to Reflection*, ed. John Beer, vol. 9 of *The Collected Works*, ed. Coburn (Princeton, 1993), p. 64, note; and *Literary Remains*, in *Complete Works*, ed. Shedd, V, 224.

We must believe in order to act, and act in order to understand our belief.

Symbol for Coleridge, as Coulson insists, has a dual function: "It points not only to the transcendent, but it is the means by which the transcendent or absolute claims or finds us. In one sense we discover symbols; but in another they discover us, as we express, embody, or perform the actions they enjoin" (p. 36).

All this is closely linked with Coulson's view that Coleridge belongs to a tradition antithetical to the Benthamite tradition that descends from Descartes. The latter is profoundly distrustful of language: language can easily deceive, and one must strive for, and trust only, ideas that are clear and distinct. The other, older tradition—to which Coleridge belongs—has a deep and abiding trust in language as the embodiment of the experiences of a community. "For him the primary response to language is not analytic, but fiduciary. In religion, as in poetry, we are required to make a complex act of inference and assent, and we begin by taking *on trust* expressions which are usually in analogical, metaphorical, or symbolic form, and by acting out the claims they make: understanding religious language is a function of understanding poetic language" (p. 4).

For Coleridge, poetry—as symbolic utterance—is not deceptive; it is, rather, the most full and exacting possible use of language. This is not because it is clear and distinct—because it defines (sets limits to) things—but precisely because it does not. A work of art is "rich in proportion to the variety of parts which it holds in unity."[21] The most successful poem or symbol is that which successfully holds in balance the widest reach of reality. Such a symbol is the work of "the poet, described in *ideal* perfection."[22] Nor

---

[21] "On Poesy or Art," *Biographia Literaria*, ed. Shawcross, II, 255. Shawcross cites Lecture XIII of 1818, following *The Literary Remains of Samuel Taylor Coleridge*, ed. Henry Nelson Coleridge, 4 vols. (London, 1836–1839), I, 216–230, as the source of this essay. It should be noted that the text of this lecture established by Foakes (*LL*, II, 217–225) does not include the phrase quoted above.

[22] *BL*, II, 15.

should we be surprised, then, to find religious ideas expressed in symbolic language: God as Father, the Spirit of God moving over the waters of chaos, Christ as Shepherd, the parables of the kingdom of heaven. What we have here, as in poetry, is "a use of language in which words do not stand for terms possessing a constant meaning but are to be seen as components in a field of force that take their value from the charge of the field *as a whole.*"[23] In Shakespearean tragedies, we do not really know what any part of the play means until the expression of the whole play has been completed.[24] In a way, of course, this is a failure of symbolic language; it fails in precision. In another way, however, it is the triumph of language; for "the diverse and apparently contradictory aspects of a complete experience are being held in the unity which is its essential character, and in terms of which it can alone be adequately communicated to us."[25] It is in this sense that such language is "fiduciary": the symbol calls us to trust that it is truly part of a whole experience of reality larger than itself.

It is only in such a tradition of language that symbolic utterance, in Coleridge's sense, is possible. Only if one can make an act of trust (of faith, love, commitment, as we have called it) in reality and in our perception of reality, only then can the process of "mutual causality" take place. With such an act of trust, what I have called the "sacramental" character of symbol can act freely. Symbolic utterance, whether in words or gestures or images, can "find" us, as Coleridge would say, and evoke a response of our whole being, leading us to even deeper perception of the reality opened up to us, both within and without.

Ultimately what is at issue here is the possibility of achieving again a "unified sensibility." This was, after all, the great glory of the earlier tradition of language in which Coulson places Coleridge—the tradition of Shakespeare,

---

[23] Coulson, p. 10.
[24] Coulson, p. 10.
[25] Coulson, p. 11.

Donne, and Milton, of the Elizabethan and Caroline theologians—when thought and feeling were at one. Before the Cartesian revolution dichotomized the human person, it was possible to perceive reality symbolically, in Coleridge's sense of the word. It was possible to perceive the wholeness of things, and for undivided humanity to respond to this wholeness with a wholeness of its own. But once Eliot's "dissociation of sensibility" had set in, the world was no longer one, as the human being was no longer one.

It was Coleridge's achievement that he saw the need to find again the unified sensibility that had been lost. And, in the final analysis, there was only one way for him to find it—through religious vision. Only when humankind could perceive the world as God perceives it, by "participating in the creative act of the infinite I AM," could we see the vision of the world's wholeness, the "translucence of the Eternal through and in the Temporal." This symbolic vision is profoundly sacramental. It is God reaching out to his people, humankind reaching out to God—"through and in the Temporal"—and encountering each other in the joy of the symbolic act.

3

The Poetry of Reference

COLERIDGE, like Wordsworth, was deeply dissatisfied with the state of poetry in his day and with the poetry of the age preceding him. The whole point of his poetic and critical endeavor was precisely to achieve again the unified sensibility that had been lost, to "redeem from mediocrity," in Auden's phrase, the poetry of his age.

J. A. Appleyard has remarked that the *Biographia Literaria*—for all the diffuseness abominated by its detractors—is essentially a unified work. It has, he says, "the structure of an argument, an attempt by Coleridge to convince himself of the unity of his literary philosophy. The two volumes are in some respects two separate versions of the same argument, the second a final effort to succeed on different grounds from these where the first failed."[1] For all the cogency of Appleyard's analysis, another view of Coleridge's aim in the *Biographia* might be taken. It does not contradict Appleyard's version, but complements it. For it might be said with equal truth that the two volumes of the *Biographia* are two parallel attempts to answer the questions, "What was wrong with the poetry of the eighteenth century?" and "How should we proceed with poetry today?"

Early in each volume Coleridge turns to the poetry of the age just past, offering a harsh judgment on it: in Chapter I, in his "Comparison between the Poets before and since Mr. Pope," and in Chapter XVI, in his "Striking points of difference between the Poets of the present age and those of the 15th and 16th centuries."[2] The first leads him directly to the burden of the first volume: the history of his own

---

[1] *Coleridge's Philosophy of Literature: The Development of a Concept of Poetry, 1791–1819* (Cambridge, Mass., 1965), p. 171.
[2] *BL*, I, 5; II, 29.

development toward realization of the unity of the human faculties; the second, to the central issue of the second volume, the reason for the superiority of Wordsworth's genius. The opening chapter has been much discussed, but the parallelism of these two chapters has not, to my knowledge, been noted; Chapter XVI, in fact, is rarely discussed, even in the most extensive analyses of the *Biographia*.[3] Yet it seems to me that Coleridge's return to this theme of the inadequacies of eighteenth-century poetry suggests a new view of his deepest concerns.

However dim a view we may now take about Coleridge's ᛁ own youthful judgments of, respectively, his admired William Lisle Bowles and the less admired Alexander Pope, we should not allow this view to obscure the deeper kind of judgment Coleridge is making about the poetry of the eighteenth century. Whatever his admiration for the "logic of wit" (I, 18) in Pope, what withholds from Pope "the legitimate name of poet" is what Coleridge calls the "conjunction disjunctive" of his poetry: "a *point* was looked for at the end of each second line, and the whole was as it were a sorites, or, if I may exchange a logical for a grammatical metaphor, a *conjunction disjunctive*, of epigrams" (I, 18–19). After a similar judgment on the poetry of Erasmus Darwin, Coleridge points his objection more sharply in a selection of two passages from Shakespeare and Gray. In Shakespeare's lines (from *The Merchant of Venice*, II, 6), Coleridge's point is, clearly, that every word tells, nothing is wasted or superfluous:

> How like a younker or a prodigal,
> The skarfed bark puts from her native bay,
> Hugg'd and embraced by the strumpet wind!
> How like the prodigal doth she return,

---

[3] There is no reference to it, for example, in the excellent studies of Appleyard (see note 1) and Richard Harter Fogle, *The Idea of Coleridge's Criticism* (Berkeley, Calif., 1962); J. V. Baker, in *The Sacred River*, makes no reference to the text of the chapter, referring only in passing to one of Coleridge's notes.

> With over-weather'd ribs and ragged sails,
> Lean, rent, and beggar'd by the strumpet wind!

Gray's "imitation" of this passage, in "The Bard," moves by fits and starts; there is no single controlling metaphor:

> Fair laughs the morn, and soft the zephyr blows,
> While proudly riding o'er the azure realm
> In gallant trim the gilded vessel goes,
> YOUTH at the prow and PLEASURE at the helm;
> Regardless of the sweeping whirlwind's sway,
> That hush'd in grim repose, expects its evening prey.

Although Coleridge comments that "I preferred the original on the ground, that in the imitation it depended wholly on the compositor's putting, or not putting, a *small Capital*, both in this, and in many other passages of the same poet, whether the words should be personifications, or mere abstractions," it becomes clear in the pages that follow that his criticism is broader than this. For he concludes that there is "one great distinction" between even the characteristic faults of the poets before Pope—he is now thinking of others than Shakespeare—and the "false beauty of the moderns": "In the former, from DONNE to COWLEY, we find the most fantastic out-of-the-way thoughts, but in the most pure and genuine mother English; in the latter, the most obvious thoughts, in language the most fantastic and arbitrary." The major fault of the "moderns" is "the glare and glitter of a perpetual, yet broken and heterogeneous imagery, or rather . . . an amphibious something, made up, half of image, and half of abstract meaning" (I, 23–24). The point at issue, therefore, is not simply one of language—"genuine mother English"—but also one of unity of viewpoint and impression. It is manifested in the choice of words, and only so manifested, but it is something beyond mere words themselves: "Our genuine admiration of a great poet is a continuous *under-current* of feeling; it is everywhere present, but seldom anywhere as a separate excitement" (I, 23).

If we turn, then, from the opening chapter directly to Chapter XVI, we may be prepared to read with a fresh eye this neglected chapter, linking (appropriately) a brief but glowing chapter on Shakespeare and the first of the famous chapters on Wordsworth. In the Shakespeare chapter Coleridge has insisted that images "become proofs of original genius only as far as they are modified by a predominant passion; or by associated thoughts or images awakened by that passion; or when they have the effect of reducing multitude to unity, or succession to an instant; or lastly, when a human and intellectual life is transferred to them from the poet's own spirit, 'which shoots its being through earth, sea, and air' " (II, 23).[4] In contrast to Shakespeare, the "poet of the present age" aims at "new and striking IMAGES" and "INCIDENTS that interest the affections or excite the curiosity." His characters and descriptions are, above all, "specific and individual, even to a degree of portraiture," but he is comparatively careless about diction and meter (II, 29). But when Coleridge returns to the poets of the fifteenth and sixteenth centuries, it becomes apparent that what most concerns him is the relationship between the parts and the whole. Their imagery is usually general: "sun, moon, flowers, breezes, murmuring streams, warbling songsters, delicious shades, lovely damsels cruel as fair, nymphs, naiads, and goddesses, are the materials which are common to all, and which each shaped and arranged according to his judgement or fancy, little solicitous to add or to particularize." The thoughts, too, "are as little novel as the images." What was important was the art, "the studied position of words and phrases, so that not only each part should be melodious in itself, but contribute to the harmony of the whole" (II, 33).

Of course, the best of the modern poets have their own virtues, virtues not shared (Coleridge felt) by the generality of *their* predecessors. If the "elder bards" had "the high finish, the appropriateness, the facility, the delicate proportion, and above all, the perfusive and omnipresent grace,"

---

[4] The quotation, slightly altered, is from Coleridge's own "France: An Ode," line 100.

the moderns have their own virtues: "the keener interest, deeper pathos, manlier reflection, and the fresher and more various imagery, which give a value and a name that will not pass away to the poets who have done honor to our own times, and to those of our immediate predecessors" (II, 35–36). The challenge of the present age is to turn to the "man of genius, who should attempt and realize a union" (II, 34). Only by such a union of virtues, Coleridge believed, could the faults of both be overcome. Shakespeare and Milton clearly stand apart, but for the rest, the earlier poets often erred by an excess of generality—sacrificing specificity to harmony of artistic form; the moderns have sacrificed both generality and harmony of form to the desire for novelty, achieved commonly through the individual, even the bizarre. Clearly, the stage is set for Coleridge's next chapter, on Wordsworth, the "man of genius" who would resolve the dilemma, the peer of Milton, the almost peer of the peerless Shakespeare. The stage is set for a new kind of poetry.

Before we turn to the new poetry, it will be helpful to ask: was Coleridge too harsh a judge of the old poetry? Probably the answer is yes. He was judging his immediate predecessors in the light of his own new vision of what poetry should be and, therefore, often not seeing their own very real excellences. To better understand this vision, let us stand for a moment in Coleridge's position and try to consider what he saw, in the light of his poetic principles. In particular, let us try the experiment of looking at eighteenth-century poetry against the background of his view of the nature of symbol, of which we have already had a preliminary view. Since the imagination is essentially the symbol-making faculty, we may ask (from this Coleridgean stance) to what extent the poetry of the eighteenth century fulfills Coleridge's idea of what constitutes symbol.

What can we expect to find in poetry of symbol? Very much, it seems, what we have just seen Coleridge lamenting the loss of in the *Biographia Literaria*. However it be manifested—in diction, meter, harmonious form, or that "continuous *under-current* of feeling" that is "everywhere present"—one must expect to find oneness. First of all, it is a unity of the experience itself, at least as it reaches us—unity that shows itself to have been achieved by a single grasp of the imagination. Secondly, it is a oneness of the poet and the object the poet experiences, in which the poet is *part* of the experience he or she portrays. Finally, where non-material reality is part of the experience, it is a oneness of matter and spirit, even of the immanent and the transcendent. Clearly, the two lines of discussion we have begun come together here: the consubstantiality of symbol—which "partakes of the reality which it renders intelligible"—and the poetic genius which has the effect of "reducing multitude to unity"—"everywhere present, but seldom anywhere as a separate excitement."

Let us take, for example, Thomson's "Hymn on Solitude" (1729), a poem not untypical of the eighteenth-century meditative tradition. It opens with a typical apostrophe:

> Hail, mildly pleasing solitude,
> Companion of the wise and good.[5]

The relationship to the poet is stated—rather baldly, it must be confessed:

> Oh! how I love with thee to walk,
> And listen to thy whisper'd talk.

What follows—almost the rest of the poem—is an exemplification, not without its charm, of the contention:

> A thousand shapes you wear with ease,
> And still in every shape you please.

Solitude is in turn a philosopher, a bird sweeping the sky, a shepherd, a sweetly passionate lover, a friend. It is morning, noon, and evening. It is a royal figure, attended by angels, virtues, and religion, by liberty and by Urania. Finally, solitude dwells in the "deep recesses" of the "oak clad hill,"

---

[5] Unless otherwise noted, all quotations from eighteenth-century poetry will be taken from *A Collection of English Poems, 1660–1800*, ed. Ronald S. Crane (New York, 1932).

and there the poet can take refuge when the sight of London in the distance—"its crimes, its cares, its pains"—becomes more than he can bear.

This is not a negligible poem, fine enough of its kind, "mildly pleasing," one might say, like solitude itself. The point here will be not that it is not good poetry, but simply that it is poetry of a particular kind. We might call it a poetry of "reference" rather than a poetry of "encounter."[6] By this I mean that it points to things—or to persons, to feelings, to spiritual realities—but it does not encounter them, or help us to encounter them. It is a poetry of metaphor, often sharp and telling, but not a poetry of symbol. In a metaphor we first are aware of the differences between the referents ("My Luve," the "red, red rose"), and then come to see some quality or qualities common to them. In symbol we first are conscious of the unity (Eliot's rose, Yeats's tree or tower), and only gradually become aware of its complexity. In Thomson's poem, the metaphors range from the slack personification of the opening apostrophe—we are never even sure of the gender of the figure of solitude—through the merely conventional ("A shepherd next, you haunt the plain, / And warble forth your oaten strain")—to the graceful and moving metaphors of the day's decline:

> But chief, when evening scenes decay,
> And the faint landskip swims away,
> Thine is the doubtful soft decline,
> And that best hour of musing thine.

But even at its best, which is very good indeed, the poem remains a skillful texture of metaphors. One does not have the sense that it was achieved by a single grasp of the imagination. It seems, rather, the elaboration of an entire series of imaginative experiences thoughtfully organized as an inductive argument. For all its emphasis on feeling, it remains a poetry of thought—thought translated, and very well trans-

---

[6] My use of the term "poetry of encounter," though similar in some ways, should not be confused with that of Frederick Garber in his valuable study *Wordsworth and the Poetry of Encounter* (Urbana, Ill., 1971).

lated—into feelings evoked by a series of imaginative experiences. In Coleridgean terms, the poem itself is the work of fancy, not of imagination.

Even the poet himself remains, in large measure, apart from his experience—perhaps precisely because he is *too* thoughtful—because his thought stands between him and his experience. He hails solitude as something apart from him; he appeals to solitude to let him "pierce thy secret cell"; he can look upon its "thousand shapes," but cannot share its life.

Finally, in the momentary glimpse of transcendent reality,

> Religion's beams around thee shine,
> And chear thy glooms with light divine,

the transcendent remains distant, apart. Light shines, but from an unseen source apart. Matter and spirit do not become one in vision; immanent and transcendent only *point* to each other. There is reference, but no encounter. There is a breach not merely between thought and feeling—Eliot's "dissociation of sensibility"—but also between the immanent and the transcendent. As Patricia Meyer Spacks writes in *The Poetry of Vision*: "In Thomson's imagery, meaning does not really inhere in the landscape; it is felt as the product of human imagination or intelligence contemplating the natural scene."[7] She goes on: when Thomson says, "Hail, Source of Being! Universal Soul / of heaven and earth!" he is "elaborating the relation between the Deity and natural process."[8] That is precisely the point, not only about the relationship between the immanent and the transcendent, but also about the relationship between the thought and the

---

[7] *The Poetry of Vision: Five Eighteenth Century Poets* (Cambridge, Mass., 1967), pp. 22–23. Ralph Cohen seems to be saying much the same when he remarks about *The Seasons*: "It was composed of diverse fragments, the purpose of which was to establish links and contrasts among nature, animals, man and God. Thus Thomson created a world of simultaneous occurrences in space, but these only occasionally led to harmonious blending." *The Unfolding of "The Seasons"* (Baltimore, 1970), pp. 326–327.

[8] The lines are from *The Seasons*, "Spring," lines 556–557.

feeling, between the poet and his experience, between the poem and the reader. These relationships must be "elaborated," precisely because they are not achieved in a single grasp of the imagination. It is metaphoric poetry, but it is not symbolic. The "poetry of vision" of which Spacks writes is, by and large, a vision of something apart, not of an immanent presence. In short, we do not find unity in the experience itself; nor do we find a deep unity between the poet and his experience; nor, finally, do we find unity of matter and spirit, of immanent and transcendent.

Considerably more skillful and more successful is William Collins's "Ode to Evening" (1747). Where Thomson's "Hymn" was in some measure disjointed—an elaborated series of metaphors rather than a single elaborated metaphor—Collins's poem is more controlled and more unified. The personified Evening is considerably more distinct in outline than Thomson's figure of solitude. Clearly a feminine figure, she is consistent throughout: "chaste Eve," "Nymph reserv'd," "Maid compos'd," "calm Vot'ress," "meekest Eve." She breathes, and evokes, a spirit of solemnity. Around her are gathered—her "return" is reminiscent of one of Spenser's great processions in *The Faerie Queene*—all the other metaphoric figures of the poem. She is not only the center of movement, but also the center of gravity. There are conventional pastoral requirements: the "oaten stop" and "pastoral song." There are the natural attributes of the countryside: springs and gales, the lake and heath and "up-land fallows." There are the figures associated with evening itself: the setting sun, the "weak-ey'd bat," the darkening vale, the "folding star arising," the elves and nymphs of night. And there are the images of the seasons: chill winds, driving rain, and swelling floods; the showers of Spring; Summer's "ling'ring light"; the "sallow Autumn" which—with breathtaking beauty—"fills thy lap with leaves." All these are arranged, with consummate artistry, around the calm figure of Evening.

There is an intricate double movement to the procession of Evening, too. It is as if there were at once two processions, two returns, taking place in two distinct, but not separate, temporal frames of reference. First of all, there is the daily return of evening, bringing its "pensive pleasures" and gently leading the poet to reflect on—what? Stillness? Then there is a concomitant but slower procession, in which Evening is linked metaphorically with the passage of seasons. She is not only the daily evening; she is the winter evening, the evening of spring, of summer, of autumn. There is no season, the poet concludes, that is not subject to her "gentlest influence."

Collins's poem is unquestionably "a miracle of rare device." It reveals the fancy working at its best, that faculty which, when it functions well, Coleridge never ceased to respect, however much he ranked it below the imagination. (The work of fancy was necessary, after all, as we shall see, even to Wordsworth, even to Shakespeare.) The metaphoric complexity of the "Ode to Evening" is totally controlled and subtly modulated, shifting easily from the movement of the day to the movement of the passing year. There is even a sense—as there is not in Thomson's "Hymn"—of a single vision. But for all this, there is again a subtle sense of a vision that has been "thought through" and then worked out poetically by a strong and creative mind. There is again the impression of a vision described rather than an experience shared. This time we feel closer to the experience, but we are not quite there. It is a poetry of reference more than of encounter.

Nor, again, are the poet and his experience truly one. Evening remains a teacher:

> Now teach me, Maid compos'd,
> To breathe some soften'd strain.

He hails her "genial lov'd return," and if she will lead he promises to follow her. But she is a figure whom he follows, not a life he shares. The gentling influence she sheds is much like Collins's "light divine": it comes from a source apart.

What Spacks feels about Thomson is equally applicable

to one of the greatest poets of the age, Thomas Gray: "meaning does not really inhere in the landscape; it is felt as the product of human imagination or intelligence contemplating the natural scene." Feeling the obvious power, though, of the "Elegy Written in a Country Church-yard" (1750), one is constrained to add that this very distance from the "meaning" may be an important part of its particular kind of power. If there is an emotional force in being drawn into an experience, there is, too, an emotional force, however different, in remaining apart from an experience and yet resonating with it. The string that vibrates sympathetically with one an octave apart from it is affected in a way no less real than the string that is tuned exactly with the original. The relationship is not better or worse, only different.

Gray's "Elegy," like Thomson's "Hymn on Solitude," is poetry of reference. It is a poem of enormous dignity and meditative pathos. In its sense of ritual and solemnity, it is in the tradition of great processional poetry. However unlike Thomson's poem in other ways, it is similar in that in neither poem does the reader enter the experience. In Gray's poem, the reader is invited to stand and watch, and to have a more perceptive eye point out the meaning of the common things we all see. It is, unashamedly, a teacher's poetry. The poet will make us see and hear it all: the tolling bell, the lowing herd, the plowman, the darkening landscape, the silent but eloquent quiet of the graveyard. And he will tell us what it means, what sermons are preached to us from this quiet world "far from the madding crowd's ignoble strife." Finally, he will draw our thoughts from the lessons of mortality to that other world where dwells "his Father and his God."

Gray touches us not because we share *his* experience, but because we are "kindred spirits" *with* him, because we have had like experience of our own. We, too, have been touched by mortality in our own lives—though tuned an octave higher or lower than he—and he has the power to evoke, through metaphors we know, the memories of our own experience. It is less the evocation of a new experience than the evocation of an experience once felt and now revived in us. In Cowper's words:

> There is in souls a sympathy with sounds,
> And as the mind is pitch'd the ear is pleas'd
> With melting airs or martial, brisk or grave.
> Some chord in unison with what we hear
> Is touched within us, and the heart replies.
>
> . . . Wherever I have heard
> A kindred melody, the scene recurs,
> And with it all its pleasures and its pains.
>   (*The Task*, Book VI)[9]

Perhaps even less in Gray than in Thomson is there the sense of oneness between the poet and his experience. This is not an accusation of falsehood or hypocrisy, but simply a realization that the poet keeps a discreet distance from his experience, that he too is watching the procession, or tapestry, with the reader. In relationship to the reader, he is a kindly guide, but he is neither an *alter ego* nor an intimate confidant. He is perhaps kin to the archetypal eighteenth-century "disinterested spectator," who commonly represents withdrawal to rural solitude as opposed to engagement in the active life. Finally, there remains an even more than discreet distance—it is rather a "great gulf fixed"—between the quiet church-yard of Stoke Poges and the "dread abode" of God. This remains poetry that metaphorically points the way, not poetry of encounter.

William Cowper's fairly typical eighteenth-century gifts make him a poet of the everyday world. He can celebrate the passage of the seasons, a "faithful bird," even such a homely object as the famous sofa; but this may be as much a limitation as a gift. It is typical of much eighteenth-century poetry that ordinary things must be "elevated" into po-

---

[9] William Cowper, *The Task*, Book VI, in *Cowper: Verse and Letters*, ed. Brian Spiller (Cambridge, Mass., 1968), pp. 514–515. All quotations from the poem will be from this edition.

etic objects. The world of poetry and the workaday world remain two distinct realms. The everyday world is not in itself "poetic." The poetry is something added, a tricking-out of common life in borrowed robes.

This brings to mind once again Eliot's much-vexed "dissociation of sensibility." The poets of the eighteenth century, he said, "thought and felt by fits, unbalanced; they reflected." [10] This is, in fact, what we have been seeing throughout this chapter—a poetry of reflection. Eliot's phrase implies a duality, the duality of not merely distinct but separate things. It suggests thought and feeling "pointing" at each other, as at something apart.

There is this same duality in even the greatest of Cowper's poems, *The Task*. What I have in mind here is not simply the catch-all nature of the poem; that is, after all, at least half the reason for its appeal. Nor am I suggesting that it is not a unified poem. Contrary to the belief of many casual readers, it is a carefully organized work. Its unity, however, is a unity of theme. His "task" is, of course, that set for him by Lady Austen, to write a blank verse poem about a sofa. But it is not long before we see that the "task" is much larger than this. It is the task facing the Christian: how to put oneself right with God and the world around one. It soon becomes clear that the beautifully detailed world the poet sets before us—the graves, the streams, the country folk,

> The air salubrious of her lofty hills,
> The chearing fragrance of her dewy vales
> And music of her woods—

are all signs of something else. As Brian Spiller puts it: "The vignettes of landscape, observed with photographic clarity of detail, are illustrations of the wholesome joys of the simple life; the comments on contemporary events are related to Cowper's view of the world; the diversions, such

---

[10] T. S. Eliot, "The Metaphysical Poets," *Selected Essays* (New York, 1932), p. 248.

as the instructions for raising cucumbers, turn out to be parables."[11]

This is a very suggestive idea. One is tempted to ask whether the whole poem is perhaps a kind of parable. This would surely be to say too much, but the analogy may be helpful. A parable, like an allegory, involves two story lines: they run parallel to each other, but do not meet; the one points to the other, but they do not share each other's life. There is a similar separation in *The Task*. The picturesque and touching details of country life point to, but are not wholly one with, the lesson they teach, that "God made the country, and man made the town." The allusions to contemporary affairs point to, but are separate from, such lessons as this:

> Sure there is need of social intercourse,
> Benevolence and peace and mutual aid
> Between the nations, in a world that seems
> To toll the death-bell of its own decease,
> And by the voice of all its elements
> To preach the gen'ral doom.
> (*The Task*, Book II, p. 419)

Perhaps we have gone too far. To be sure, there is much in Cowper that is typical of the century. There is the same sense of a "discreet distance" between the poet and the reader; there is a similar sense of distance between immanent and transcendent reality—though it is a far cry from the deist's distancing of God, which Cowper rejects so movingly in the last book of his poem:

> One spirit—His
> Who wore the platted thorns with bleeding brows,
> Rules universal nature. Not a flow'r
> But shows some touch in freckle, streak or stain,
> Of his unrivall'd pencil.
> (*The Task*, Book VI, p. 521)

But in Cowper the unity of the experience itself is something else again. For all his typicality in certain ways, Cow-

---

[11] Spiller, p. 394.

per is a poet of transition. Of all the eighteenth-century poets, not only is he (after Pope) the most considerable poet, but he is also (with Christopher Smart) the closest in spirit to the new poetry soon to be born.

We have spoken of the unity of *The Task* as essentially a unity of theme. Yet with Cowper one hesitates: there is something more. What draws us back to the poem is not simply the graceful ease of the verse, the simplicity of diction, the charm of the rural descriptions. It is the man himself, glimpsed and heard within and between the lines. If there is here, as in so much eighteenth-century poetry, a distance between the immanent and the transcendent and between the poet and his experience—as we said of Thomson, his thought often seems to stand between him and his experience—there is also something different: a remarkable oneness of vision, an awareness of the poet himself. He may be "thinking and feeling by fits," but we sense that it is one man doing both. We are not surprised to find Coleridge saying of Cowper—along with Coleridge's beloved William Lisle Bowles—that they were "to the best of my knowledge, the first who combined natural thoughts with natural diction; the first who reconciled the heart with the head."[12] With Cowper we have begun to move at least into the gravitational pull of a new poetic world, in which the poet reveals himself more fully and more freely to his reader.

It is possible that what this experiment proves, of reading eighteenth-century poetry in terms of Coleridgean principles, is the limitation of those principles. This is, in fact, borne out by what we have seen of Coleridge's strictures against "modern poets" in the *Biographia*. There is surely considerable blindness in his view of eighteenth-century poetry. For one thing, he often seems to ignore its range and variety. It is a rare moment when he bothers to distinguish even the broadest kinds of poetry of his predecessors—the poetry of wit, for example, from the poetry of sentiment. One of these rare moments is in a manuscript memorandum

---

[12] *BL*, I, 25.

(from about 1796) for a proposed "History of English Poetry." He distinguishes there between "Dryden and . . . the witty Logicians" (with whom he includes not only Pope, but also Ben Jonson, Donne, and Cowley) and "Modern Poetry," by which he means Cowper, Burns, Thomson, Collins, Akenside, and others.[13] More commonly, though, his adversary is simply (as in the *Biographia*) "the Poets since Mr. Pope," including Pope himself. Their sin is, at bottom, that they are not Wordsworth.

In the work of these "adversaries" Coleridge had no very real sense, for example, of the value of "decorum"—as in Pope—being as preoccupied as he is with its hardening into mere stereotype in many of their successors. He was not sensitive to the subtle possibilities of the couplet, so concerned was he with the fluid and organic movement of the whole poem. He did not fully appreciate that there could be an intensity of wit, so taken was he with the need for intensity of vision. So enamored was he with the personal and visionary intensity of Wordsworth that he had difficulty seeing the often statuesque or processional beauties of Gray. Nor did he seem aware how much the poets of the later eighteenth century were themselves struggling, often successfully, against neo-classical restraints, trying to shake off (in W. Jackson Bate's memorable phrase) "the burden of the past."

For all his myopia about the very real excellences of eighteenth-century poetry, however, Coleridge did see something important about its limitations. Struggling though it was, that poetry had not yet, except in fleeting moments, broken free from its essentially referential mode. It was like the statue breaking out of the marble. With Cowper it was almost there—the transcendent, the world of nature, the deeply personal—almost touching, almost meeting. In Wordsworth, it will have broken free, into that "unity of being in which all the usual distinctions—objective and subjective, man and nature, intellect and feeling, conscious and

---

[13] *Inquiring Spirit*, ed. Kathleen Coburn (London, 1951), p. 153.

unconscious"—are seen as "only aspects or modes of the whole."[14]

In any relationship of poetic son and father there is a deep ambiguity. Coleridge was not always, or entirely, blind to the beauties of the eighteenth-century poets. There are moments when he can look back at them with affection, for all their differences from him. In a remarkable letter to his friend John Thelwall on December 17, 1796—which cannot help but call to mind again Eliot's view that eighteenth-century poets "thought and felt by fits, unbalanced"— Coleridge suggests that he was writing a different kind of poetry from his immediate predecessors. "I feel strongly, and I think strongly; but I seldom feel without thinking or think without feeling. . . . My philosophical opinions are blended with, or deduced from, my feelings: and this, I think, peculiarizes my style of Writing. And like every thing else, it is sometimes a beauty and sometimes a fault." Yet this view of a new and different poetry still left him free (at least for the moment) to admire what he felt were the very different beauties of poets before him, for he continues: "But do not let us introduce an act of Uniformity against Poets—I have room enough in *my* brain to admire, aye and almost equally, the *head* and fancy of Akenside, and the *heart* and fancy of Bowles, the solemn Lordliness of Milton, and the divine Chit chat of Cowper."[15] The excitement of the poetry of encounter did not make him lose entirely his taste for the more restrained beauties of the poetry of reference.

---

[14] W. Jackson Bate, *The Burden of the Past and the English Poet* (Cambridge, Mass., 1970), p. 125.
[15] *CL*, I, 279.

4

The Poetry of Encounter:
Wordsworth

WHAT IS STILL COMMONLY TAKEN as the manifesto of the "new poetry"—Wordsworth's Preface to the second edition of the *Lyrical Ballads* in 1800—hardly gets to the nub of the matter. Of course, it is a manifesto: for all its reassuring denials that the reader is being asked to embrace new friends "only upon condition of his abandoning his old friends,"[1] it is clearly flinging down the gauntlet before the poets of the old style. The title page of the new second volume of 1800 bears the motto: "Quam nihil ad genium, Papiniane, tuum!"—which might be loosely translated "Follower of Pope, this will hardly be to *your* liking!"

In many ways the famous Preface remains important and suggestive, and yet it often leads on a false scent, because— after the opening few paragraphs—it becomes excessively preoccupied with the matters of subject ("incidents of common life") and of diction (the language of "low and rustic life").[2] There will be "no personifications of abstract ideas in these volumes" (p. 250); the poet will use "the very language of men" (p. 250); and there will be "little of what is usually called poetic diction" (p. 251). Further, it will be seen in these poems that there is "no essential difference between the language of prose and metrical composition" (p. 253), and yet meter will help in "tempering and restraining the passion by an intertexture of ordinary feeling" (p. 264).

---

[1] William Wordsworth and Samuel Taylor Coleridge, *Lyrical Ballads: The Text of the 1798 Edition with the Additional 1800 Poems and the Prefaces*, ed. R. L. Brett and A. R. Jones (London, 1963), p. 271.

[2] *Lyrical Ballads*, pp. 244–245.

But all this is not what Wordsworth's "new poetry" is most deeply about. The crucial element is not merely a change in technique, significant though this is, but a change in vision. What is at issue is indicated not so much by what Wordsworth says about diction as by the reasons he gives for his innovative subjects and techniques. What is important is not that he uses "low and rustic life," but that he does so "because in that situation the passions of men are incorporated with the beautiful and permanent forms of nature" (p. 245); not that he chooses subjects that manifest "moral sensations" common to men—he refers us to poems like "The Idiot Boy," "We are Seven," "Simon Lee," and "Poor Susan"—but that "the feeling therein developed gives importance to the action and situation and not the action and situation to the feeling" (p. 248); not his firm determination to purify poetic diction, but his realization of the strong bond that exists between humankind and the rest of the world—his "deep impression of certain inherent and indestructible qualities of the human mind, and likewise of certain powers in the great and permanent objects that act upon it which are equally inherent and indestructible" (pp. 249–250). Even more significant than Wordsworth's revolution in poetic technique is his revolution in poetic vision—a vision of the deep and inherent interrelationships of thought and feeling, of mind and nature, of nature and the transcendent.

To witness this revolution in poetic vision, however, we must turn to Wordsworth's poetry, and to theorize about it we must turn to Coleridge. It is Coleridge who cared about the theory—or, we might say, the implications—of this new poetry. It is futile to look to Wordsworth's Preface for more than fitful light; as he himself said in later years, he "never cared a straw about the theory, and the Preface was written at the request of Mr. Coleridge out of sheer good nature."[3]

---

[3] *Times Literary Supplement* (London), April 28, 1950, p. 261; quoted in Paul M. Zall, ed., *Literary Criticism of William Wordsworth*, Regents Critics Series (Lincoln, Neb., 1966), p. 15.

Not only was the Preface written "at the request of Mr. Coleridge," but it clearly represents Coleridge's thought at least as much as Wordsworth's. Coleridge was not indulging in self-puffery when he wrote to Robert Southey in 1802 that the Preface is "half a child of my own Brain & so arose out of Conversations, so frequent, that with few exceptions we could scarcely either of us perhaps positively say, which first started any particular Thought." But the burden of Coleridge's comments to Southey is that he is "far from going all lengths with Wordsworth," that, on the contrary, he suspects that "some where or other there is a radical Difference in our theoretical opinions respecting Poetry."[4] Unlike many of his promises, Coleridge's resolve that "this I shall endeavor to go to the bottom of" was destined to be fulfilled, at least in part. It was not until 1815—and it might be said that even then he never quite got to the "bottom" of the matter—but the second volume of the *Biographia Literaria* goes a long way toward fulfilling that promise.

For many critics, the six chapters on Wordsworth (Chapters XIV, XVII–XX, XXII) are the real heart of the *Biographia Literaria*. This may be heresy for those of us who take a more organic view of the *Biographia*—and who therefore feel that these chapters can be fully appreciated only within the context of Coleridge's entire argument—but there is little question that the chapters on Wordsworth are examples of Coleridge's practical criticism at its best. Even beyond this, it can be argued that it is here that we find the clearest view of his poetic theory as well, implicit in his judgments on the greatest poet of his age. Here we can see—at least more clearly than in the Wordsworth/Coleridge Preface to the *Lyrical Ballads*—what essentially characterized the new poetry, seen in the work of its greatest practitioner. Coleridge has now had fifteen years of reflection on the meaning of the phenomenon of Wordsworth, and the passage of time has given him distance to see what is most deeply at issue.

---

[4] *CL*, II, 830.

Coleridge begins (Chapter XIV) with the division of labor between himself and Wordsworth in the *Lyrical Ballads*: his own to be poems of the supernatural, Wordsworth to treat subjects "chosen from ordinary life." He then offers a preliminary view of his idea of a poem and of poetry—the first leading to a brief discussion of the organic nature of a poem ("the parts of which mutually support and explain each other" and which moves "like the motion of a serpent"),[5] the second to the classic description of "the poet, described in ideal perfection," to which we have referred earlier (II, 15–16). This is only preliminary, though, to the lengthy analysis of Wordsworth's poetry in the chapters to come (Chapters XVII–XX, XXII). It is there that the lines will be drawn, that he will "declare once for all, in what points I coincide with his opinions, and in what points I altogether differ" (II, 10).

The differences are, in the last analysis, relatively superficial. True, Coleridge does detail at some length (Chapters XVII–XX) his disagreements with Wordsworth on the choice of "low and humble subjects" and on the matter of an essential difference between "the language of prose and metrical composition"—and in the process offers some of his most perceptive criticism. And Coleridge does go on (Chapter XXII) to outline what he considers the "characteristic defects" of Wordsworth's poetry. But what is important for us here are not the differences between them, but the fact that in the rest of Chapter XXII (II, 142–159)—in which Coleridge discusses the characteristic "excellences" of Wordsworth's poetry—he is able to articulate what is new and exciting in this new kind of poetry.

Even here, at first, it might seem that Coleridge is following Wordsworth in his emphasis on diction, for the first of the six "excellences" he singles out is "an austere purity of language both grammatically and logically; in short a perfect appropriateness of the words to the meaning." But it soon becomes evident that Coleridge has something deeper

---

[5] *BL*, II, 13–14.

in mind: "Be it observed, however, that I include in the *meaning* of a word not only its correspondent object, but likewise all the associations which it recalls. For language is framed to convey not the object alone, but likewise the character, mood and intentions of the person who is representing it" (II, 142). Clearly, one of Wordsworth's virtues is in bringing together, in his poem, himself and the world he writes about.

Wordsworth's second virtue is said to be "a correspondent weight and sanity of the Thoughts and Sentiments, won—not from books, but—from the poet's own meditative observation" (II, 144–145). Again, the reason for this is what is most important. Wordsworth's thoughts and sentiments have a "correspondent weight and sanity"—which latter I take to mean something like "wholeness"—because they are "drawn up from depths which few in any age are priviledged [*sic*] to visit, into which few in any age have courage or inclination to descend" (II, 146–147). His poetry has "weight" and "sanity" because the deepest wells he taps are those within himself—and these are wells neither easily tapped nor easily channeled to others. To tap them deeply demands a new mode of perception; to channel them to others requires a new kind of poetry. The great "Immortality Ode," Coleridge goes on, "was intended for such readers only as had been accustomed to watch the flux and reflux of their inmost natures, to venture at times into the twilight realms of consciousness, and to feel a deep interest in modes of inmost being, to which they know that the attributes of time and space are inapplicable and alien, but which yet can not be conveyed save in symbols of time and space" (II, 147). The mysteries of poetry are no longer, first of all, the external mysteries of sea and mountain or even of God—which can be distanced and so made manageable—but the inner mysteries of the self.

The next of Wordsworth's virtues, which Coleridge merely notes almost in passing, is unambiguously a matter of diction: "the sinewy strength and originality of single lines and paragraphs: the frequent curiosa felicitas of his diction" (II, 148).

The fourth takes us again more deeply into Wordsworth: "the perfect truth of nature in his images and descriptions as taken immediately from nature" (II, 148). Coleridge exemplifies beautifully what he means: the skating scene from *The Prelude*, in which "the leafless trees and every icy crag / Tinkled like iron"; the green linnet, "perched in ecstasies" upon "Yon tuft of hazel trees / That twinkle to the gusty breeze." Coleridge comments: "Like the moisture or the polish on a pebble, genius neither distorts nor false-colours its objects; but on the contrary brings out many a vein and many a tint, which escape the eye of common observation" (II, 148). But, again, the reason: what is it that makes possible such "perfect truth of nature"? It is "a long and genial intimacy with the very spirit which gives the physiognomic expression to all the works of nature" (II, 148). Clearly, we are back to what Coleridge called "the one Life within us and abroad."

It will perhaps be evident by now that the movement of Coleridge's analysis of Wordsworth's excellences is not from one discrete virtue to another, but deeper and deeper into the center of Wordsworth's poetic vision. The movement of thought is itself almost a poetic movement—even a symbolic movement—leaving nothing behind, but taking everything with it, snowballing with the accretion of meaning. The fifth virtue of Wordsworth's poetry makes this quite clear, for it takes up into itself everything of importance that has been said before, and goes beyond it. The fifth characteristic is

a meditative pathos, a union of deep and subtle thought with sensibility; a sympathy with man as man; the sympathy indeed of a contemplator, rather than a fellow-sufferer or co-mate, (spectator, haud particeps) but of a contemplator, from whose view no difference of rank conceals the sameness of the nature; no injuries of wind or weather, or toil, or even of ignorance, wholly disguise the human face divine. The superscription and the image of the creator still remain legi-

ble to *him* under the dark lines, with which guilt or calamity
had cancelled or cross-barred it. Here the man and the poet
lose and find themselves in each other, the one as glorified,
the latter as substantiated." (II, 150)

With all that has gone before, there is now the sense of a
transcendent reality beyond, yet not beyond: the "human
face divine."

Finally, there is the triumphant claim for Wordsworth to
the surpassing power that gives him access to all the rest:
"Last, and pre-eminently, I challenge for this poet the gift
of IMAGINATION in the highest and strictest sense of the
word" (II, 151). And, clearly, from the examples Coleridge
offers—including passages from "Yew-Trees," "Resolution
and Independence," and the "Immortality Ode"—we are
back again with "the poet, described in ideal perfection,"
the poet as the focal point of poetic unity. The "whole soul
of man" is brought into activity, "with the subordination of
its faculties to one another," and thereby comes "a tone and
spirit of unity that blends, and (as it were) *fuses*, each into
each." It is a unity that is commensurate with, even demands, "the balance or reconciliation of opposite or discordant qualities": sameness and difference; general and
concrete; idea and image; the individual and the representative; novelty and familiarity; emotion and order; judgment
and feeling; the natural and the artificial; the poet and his
poem. In all this—and therefore in Wordsworth, who is pre-
eminently the poet of imagination—it is imagination that is
"the SOUL that is every where, and in each; and forms all
into one graceful and intelligent whole" (II, 16–18).

There is indeed, in both Coleridge and Wordsworth, a
new poetic vision—and a vision in a double sense: the vision out of which a poem comes into being, and the vision
of the poetic process itself—representing both the cognitive
and the ontological reach of the imagination. It is, in both
senses, a vision from which nothing seems to be left out:
the poet, his thoughts and feelings, the world of humankind
and the world of nature, the world of universal values—

whatever the human mind can know. Finally, it is a vision that demands the fusion of all these things, the transubstantiation—or, more accurately for the theologian as for Coleridge, the consubstantiation—into a new being. We may call this new being, as Coleridge does, a symbol, a poetic entity that remains consubstantial with the many realities of which it is the conductor. We are in the realm of a new poetry.

We might begin with two of Wordsworth's poems not far apart in time but far distant in poetic technique and vision. The first, "Lines Left upon a Seat in a Yew-Tree," was completed in 1795; the second, "A Night-Piece," was written in 1798. It is no mere whim that finds Wordsworth—in his otherwise often whimsical or arbitrary final arrangement of his poems—classifying the first of these with his "Poems Written in Youth," the other with "Poems of the Imagination." Although only three years apart in time, they are worlds apart in other ways. One might argue about the reason for this—surely the *annus mirabilis* with Coleridge will be one decisive factor—but the fact of the difference is clear.

"Lines Left upon a Seat in a Yew-Tree" is a poem of another age, the age just past. Despite the differences in formal structure, it has a striking affinity with Gray's "Elegy." Here again the poet is a companionable guide, bidding the reader pause for a moment in a hallowed spot, to rest and to reflect: "Nay, Traveller, rest." Again the scene is set, less in detail but no less picturesquely:

> This lonely Yew-tree stands
> Far from all human dwelling: what if here
> No sparkling rivulet spread the verdant herb?
> What if the bee love not these barren boughs?
> Yet, if the wind breathe soft, the curling waves,
> That break upon the shore, shall lull thy mind
> By one soft impulse saved from vacancy.[6]

---

[6] Quotations from Wordsworth's poetry, except for *The Prelude*, will be taken from the Oxford Standard Authors text, *Wordsworth: Poetical Works*, ed. Thomas Hutchinson, revised by Ernest de Selincourt (London, 1950).

To this are added details of the "mossy sod," "this aged Tree" taught "with its dark arms to form a circling bower," a "straggling sheep," the "glancing sand-piper." Then there is—like Gray's gifted "Youth to Fortune and to Fame Unknown"—the "youth by science nursed," a "favoured Being, knowing no desire / Which genius did not hallow." Gray's young man was never exposed to the world, and so never achieved his rightful fame; Wordsworth's youth was briefly loosed on the world, but his genius went unrecognized and he retired, in wounded pride, to the solitude of the yew-tree. In each case, the central figure is an object-lesson for the reader—the passing Stranger, like ourselves—in Gray a lesson of resignation, in Wordsworth a lesson of humility:

> Stranger! henceforth be warned; and know that pride,
> Howe'er disguised in its own majesty,
> Is littleness.

We are still with the poetry of reference. The poet is contemplating a scene, picturesque in its combination of beauty and melancholy. It is a scene that he can put to good use, as Gray does the beautiful and melancholy church-yard at Stoke Poges. The poet points out, often movingly, what is relevant to his lesson:

> And on these barren rocks, with fern and heath,
> And juniper and thistle, sprinkled o'er,
> Fixing his downcast eye, he many an hour
> A morbid pleasure nourished, tracing here
> An emblem of his own unfruitful life.

An emblem—a fitting word for this kind of poetry itself. An emblem is perhaps the most discreet and modest kind of metaphor, keeping a respectful distance from its referent. And so the poet. It is not *his* experience; nor are we really encouraged to think it is. He remains the pointer, the teacher, who says, "Look at this and learn from it."

By 1798, only three years later, Wordsworth had moved into another world of poetry, new in diction, new in imagery, new in vision. His short poem "A Night-Piece" is an admirable example.

> —The sky is overcast
> With a continuous cloud of texture close,
> Heavy and wan, all whitened by the Moon,
> Which through that veil is indistinctly seen,
> A dull, contracted circle, yielding light
> So feebly spread that not a shadow falls,
> Chequering the ground—from rock, plant, tree, or tower.
> At length a pleasant instantaneous gleam
> Startles the pensive traveller while he treads
> His lonesome path, with unobserving eye
> Bent earthwards; he looks up—the clouds are split
> Asunder,—and above his head he sees
> The clear Moon, and the glory of the heavens.
> There in a black-blue vault she sails along,
> Followed by multitudes of stars, that, small
> And sharp, and bright, along the dark abyss
> Drive as she drives: how fast they wheel away,
> Yet vanish not!—the wind is in the tree,
> But they are silent;—still they roll along
> Immeasurably distant; and the vault,
> Build round by those white clouds, enormous clouds,
> Still deepens its unfathomable depth.
> At length the Vision closes; and the mind,
> Not undisturbed by the delight it feels,
> Which slowly settles into peaceful calm,
> Is left to muse upon the solemn scene.

The focus of the poem is almost entirely—at least so it seems at first—on the sky. It is at first a muted sky, wan with the feeble light of a cloud-veiled moon, so feeble it cannot even cast a shadow. The only reference to the earth below it, except for the momentary glimpse of the earth-bound "pensive traveller," is by indirection: no shadows chequer the ground "—from rock, plant, tree, or tower." The dominant movement of the poem is the movement of the clouds: at first they are "of texture close"; then they "split asunder," opening up the view of the moon and "the glory of the heavens"; they act as a frame for the "black-blue vault" of the sky, "built round by those white clouds, enormous clouds"; and, finally, it is suggested, they close again as "the Vision closes."

Equally important, though, is the interplay of light and dark. First there is the feeble light of the veiled moon, a "dull, contracted circle." This gives way to "a pleasant instantaneous gleam" that catches the attention of the traveler's "unobserving eye." This leads him to look up to "the Vision"—"the glory of the heavens," itself compounded of light and dark. Here the light and the dark are the extremes: the dark is the awesome "black-blue vault" that is a "dark abyss"; the light is the "sharp" and "bright" light of the "multitudes of stars." Here, too, there is movement, the silent movement of the stars, "immeasurably distant," through the "unfathomable depth" of the dark vault.

These are not the only interrelationships in the poem. The clouds and the light and dark are in turn deliberately set in relationship to the world below them—rock, plant, tree, tower, and above all the traveler. As the poem unfolds, we become more and more aware that the traveler himself may be, in fact, the center of the poem. Before he appears (line 9), we are not aware of any personal viewer of the scene except ourselves. We are led directly into the scene, as if it were our own. When the traveler appears, awakened to the scene above him, it is as if we are already present and he has joined us. We are not apart from him; we share his experience, as he shares ours. This is surely one of the most important achievements of the poem: even though there is no first-person reference to encourage us to "pretend" we are the poet, we feel—and increasingly so as the poem unfolds—that we are experiencing the very sensations of the traveler. We are within the experience.

What is the experience through which we move? One might be tempted to say it is a passage from darkness to light. But no. It is, rather, a passage from indistinctness to clarity—from the feeble light of the veiled moon to the sharp dichotomies of light and dark—and at the same time a passage from inattention ("the unobserving eye") to "the Vision."

And yet, in a poem that suggests at least as much as it says, one is led to ask if there is not still another movement. Is there not a gradual journey *inward*? As the Vision closes, it is not only the sky that settles again, it is the mind's delight that "slowly settles into peaceful calm." It is the mind that has experienced the Vision—a vision of the sharp clarities of the darkness and the light, eternally related in the vastness of mystery, immeasurable, unfathomable. No wonder there is ambiguity in the response to this mystery; no wonder the mind is "not undisturbed by the delight it feels." It is the mind that has experienced the moment of mystery. We who have shared this experience have been led, too, inexorably inward. When we are left at last within the mind—to "muse upon the solemn scene"—we are not altogether sure we have ever been out of it. Was the "Vision" of something without or of something within: of a vision in the sky or of a vision of the mystery of the human mind, or somehow of both? Have the clouds and the light and the dark abyss—without ceasing to be clouds and light and the black night—become something more than themselves? In a sense, everything has been set in relationship to everything else: the clouds and the moon to inanimate and living things on earth; the clouds and the light of the stars to the black vault of night; the wind and the stars in motion harmonious with each other. As more and more parts of the experience are set in relation to the black vault above, we realize that it is the black vault above that contains them all—the vault that continues to "deepen its unfathomable depth." This dark vault has become the mind, which contains all this mystery—the mind of the traveler, the mind of the poet, our mind. The vision into which we have been led is a vision of mystery.

That is perhaps part of the secret of this new poetry: we have been led into the poet's vision of mystery. Both elements are crucial. First of all, we have been led into the poet's vision: it is, therefore, a poetry of encounter within which we truly encounter the poet and the world of his poem. He has ushered us into the process of his experience, so that we share its very unfolding. Secondly, it is a vision of mystery, and mystery can be expressed most adequately—though never completely—by symbol, not by the clarities, however richly complex they be, of metaphor alone. Symbol leaves the mystery intact. Further, these elements taken together—the encounter and the mystery—may take us even closer to the secret of the new poetry. Precisely because symbol is not hard and sharp and clear—because it, rather, suggests, intimates, provokes—it draws things (including us, if we allow ourselves to be drawn) into itself. A symbol is, to use the homely figure, a rolling snowball, taking up into itself everything it meets. A symbol does not allow us to stand apart and look on, to have things pointed out to us, but draws us into the experience of itself, which is at the same time an experience of the poet and of the poet's world. Poetry of symbol is necessarily a "poetry of encounter."

We have said often enough that for Coleridge symbol is the product of the imagination, the "symbol-making faculty." It is time perhaps to face up to a corollary of this fact that has been implicit in our discussion for some time. I mean the relationship between the metaphor/symbol distinction and the distinction of fancy and imagination. Although Coleridge nowhere says so explicitly—and it would no doubt be rash to make an easy equation between them—there can be no doubt that there is an implicit correspondence between these two distinctions.

The poetic imagination fuses disparate things into a new unity; "it dissolves, diffuses, dissipates, in order to recreate."[7] Its product is the symbol, which is characterized in the first instance, for the poet as for the reader, by unity, whose complexity is only gradually revealed; the result of this perception is a sense of mystery. "Fancy, on the con-

---

[7] *BL*, I, 304.

trary, has no other counters to play with, but fixities and definites" (I, 202). Its product is "mere metaphor," which is characterized most immediately by its duality or multiplicity of reference, and whose unity sooner or later comes to be perceived; the result is a poetry essentially more clear and definite than it is mysterious. Imagination "fuses," to use Coleridge's words, while fancy merely "aggregates."

This said, however, we must hasten to disavow any total divorce of imagination and fancy. To distinguish is not necessarily to separate. If it is clear throughout Coleridge's thought that imagination and fancy are as distinct as symbol and mere metaphor, and distinct in the same ways, it is equally clear that they often work together in the same poem. This is seen nowhere more clearly than in a passage of the *Biographia* that is bent on strongly defending the distinction between the two faculties. When Wordsworth objected (in his Preface of 1815) to Coleridge's definition of fancy as the "aggregative and associative power"— insisting that "to aggregate and to associate, to evoke and to combine, belong as well to the imagination as to the fancy"—Coleridge rejoined sharply in the *Biographia Literaria*:

> I reply, that if by the power of evoking and combining, Mr. W[ordsworth] means the same as, and no more than, I meant by the aggregative and associative, I continue to deny, that it belongs at all to the imagination; and I am disposed to conjecture, that he has mistaken the co-presence of fancy with imagination for the operation of the latter singly. A man may work with two very different tools at the same moment; each has its share in the work, but the work effected by each is distinct and different. (I, 194)

For Coleridge, there are poems aplenty that remain poetry of fancy alone, but there is no poem—at least no poem of any length—that fulfills his idea of an imaginative poem, that does not also contain poetry of fancy. "Genius must have talent as its complement and implement, just as, in like manner, imagination must have fancy. In short, the higher intellectual powers can only act through a corresponding energy of the lower."[8]

Probably the most famous instance of Coleridge's assertion of the coexistence of fancy and imagination in a single poem—made famous by I. A. Richards's lengthy discussion of it[9]—is in his notes on Shakespeare's *Venus and Adonis*. "We have shewn that [Shakespeare] possessed fancy," Coleridge says, calling it the faculty of "bringing together images dissimilar in the main by some one point or more of likeness distinguished."[10] In support of his claim Coleridge refers us to the image of Venus tenderly detaining Adonis:

> Full gently now she takes him by the hand,
> A lily prison'd in a gaol of snow.
> Or ivory in an alabaster band;
> So white a friend engirts so white a foe.[11]

But there is evidence of another faculty at work. "Still mounting, we find undoubted proof in his mind of imagination, or the power by which one image or feeling is made to modify many others and by a sort of *fusion to force many into one*—that which after shewed itself in such might and energy in *Lear*, where the deep anguish of a father spreads the feeling of ingratitude and cruelty over the very elements of heaven."[12] It should be clear from the examples Coleridge has given already that the one is poetry of metaphor alone—images "aggregated" but not "fused"—the other poetry of symbol, in which the cruelty of a daughter's ingratitude is no longer distinct from the mysterious ingratitude of the heavens, and indeed of the whole world gone mad in which Lear finds himself.

The corresponding example from *Venus and Adonis*—

---

[8] *Table Talk*, ed. Carl Woodring, vol. 14 of *The Complete Works*, ed. Coburn, 2 vols. (Princeton, 1990), I, 426 (August 17, 1833). This will be cited hereafter as *TT*.

[9] *Coleridge on Imagination*, pp. 76–84.

[10] *LL*, I, 81; see also I, 67.

[11] *Venus and Adonis*, lines 361–364.

[12] *LL*, I, 81; italics in the original.

Coleridge's example of the work of imagination in the poem—should now simply confirm this assertion that Coleridge's distinction between fancy and imagination—the immediate point of his discussion—implicitly distinguishes at the same time poetry of mere metaphor from poetry that goes beyond metaphor to become poetry of symbol. It is "the flight of Adonis from the enamoured goddess in the dusk of the evening—

> 'Look! how a bright star shooteth from the sky,
> So glides he in the night from Venus' eye.' "

The symbolic character is highlighted by Coleridge's comment: "How many images and feelings are here brought together without effort and without discord—the beauty of Adonis—the rapidity of his flight—the yearning yet hopelessness of the enamoured gazer—and a shadowy ideal character thrown over the whole."[13] There is metaphor here, to be sure—Adonis is compared to a star—but for Coleridge this is no "*mere* metaphor." The points of comparison are not clearly definable, like the band of alabaster and the "gaol of snow." Coleridge must grope to express them—beauty, rapidity, yearning—and finally admit his inability to encompass the mystery expressed by the symbol. It must remain as undefined as "a shadowy ideal character thrown over the whole," like the cruelty of Lear's dark world. Symbol must remain in mystery.

For all the distinction, however, and for all the priority given to imagination and to symbol, it is important to keep in mind that Coleridge never undervalued the work of the fancy. There is good poetry written under the aegis of the fancy, as is clear from Coleridge's admiration of some of the better eighteenth-century poets. There is poetry of fancy, too, that contains imaginative elements—as we have suggested, for example, in the work of Collins and Cowper. In any case, fancy at its best is a respectable poetic faculty that operates under rules of its own. It has a role to play

---

[13] *LL*, I, 81; the passage quoted is *Venus and Adonis*, lines 815–816.

even in poetry of the imagination. No poet works always, or completely, at full stretch. Neither he nor his readers could bear it for long. Poetry of the imagination—even the best poetry—is compounded of imagination and fancy, of symbol and metaphor.

Returning now to Wordsworth, we find this as true of him as it is of Shakespeare. His poetry is the work of both fancy and imagination and, therefore, is made up both of metaphor and of symbol. In the very moment of claiming for Wordsworth the gift of imagination "in the highest and strictest sense of the word," Coleridge explicitly claims for him, too, the lesser gift of fancy.[14] As we have said, fancy operates under rules of its own, and to Coleridge's mind Wordsworth is clearly more successful in his use of imagination than in his use of fancy. "In the play of *Fancy*, Wordsworth, to my feelings, is not always graceful, and sometimes *recondite*. The *likeness* is occasionally too strange, or demands too peculiar a point of view, or is such as appears the creature of predetermined research, rather than spontaneous presentation."[15] The product of fancy, it is implied, must be graceful, with something of a sense of spontaneity about it, and relatively clear in its references. The work of imagination—it may be inferred from Coleridge's examples in the following passage and from what he says elsewhere—will be intense, more weighty and universal, and the range of its reference will remain ultimately open-ended and mysterious.

It would be easy enough, but scarcely profitable, to instance Wordsworth's unsuccessful poetry of fancy. It will be more to the point to see fancy at work successfully in a poem of the imagination, and to see how it does its work within the context of the whole.

"Resolution and Independence" opens with a simple juxtaposition of images—hardly even metaphors yet—that are in tune with the poet's joy in nature.

---

[14] *BL*, II, 151.
[15] *BL*, II, 151; italics in the original.

> There was a roaring in the wind all night;
> The rain came heavily and fell in floods;
> But now the sun is rising calm and bright;
> The birds are singing in the distant woods;
> Over his own sweet voice the Stock-dove broods;
> The Jay makes answer as the Magpie chatters;
> And all the air is filled with pleasant noise of waters.

The humanization of nature, so far merely suggested, now
continues more explicitly.

> All things that love the sun are out of doors;
> The sky rejoices in the morning's birth;
> The grass is bright with raindrops;—on the moors
> The hare is running races in her mirth;
> And with her feet she from the plashy earth
> Raises a mist; that, glittering in the sun,
> Runs with her all the way, wherever she doth run.

As this humanization takes place, we become aware that the
poet has begun, however unconsciously, to work metaphorically: the sky's "rejoicing"; the "birth" of the morning; the
hare's "mirth"; the "running" of the mist in company with
the hare. The metaphorical mode continues as the traveler
enters the scene: he is suddenly a "boy," a "happy child of
earth"; he is set in relationship to "these blissful creatures."
In memory, "life's business" is seen as "a summer mood."
With the darkening of his mood the dead poets Chatterton
and Burns become metaphors of the poet's self. The old
leech-gatherer himself, in his first appearance, is described
metaphorically as a huge stone "couched on the bald top of
an eminence" and "a sea-beast crawled forth . . . to sun
itself." Here is everything that could be asked of a poetry
of fancy: graceful, spontaneous-seeming —both in joy and
in gloom—and clear in its reference.

Yet, with the introduction of the figure of the old man,
something has already begun to change. The old man, even
as he is compared to a stone and a sea-beast, is a figure of
mystery, a "wonder to all who do the same espy." This old
man *seems*—not so much *is*—as *seems*. A stone, he yet

seems "a thing endued with sense." He seems "not all alive nor dead, / Nor all asleep." Upon his bent frame lies "a more than human weight." Metaphor does not cease entirely—he stands "motionless as a cloud"—but more is suggested than metaphor alone can carry. For he is, too, a figure of contradictions: neither alive nor dead; human but more than human; rude in appearance but "of a lofty utterance"; weak yet somehow strong and resolute.[16]

As the poem continues, and as the relationship between the poet and the old man becomes deeper and more intense, it is evident that the old man has become more than merely himself.

> The old Man still stood talking by my side;
> But now his voice to me was like a stream
> Scarce heard; nor word from word could I divide;
> And the whole body of the Man did seem
> Like one whom I had met with in a dream;
> Or like a man from some far region sent,
> To give me human strength, by apt admonishment.

The old leech-gatherer has become a part of the poet—at least of the poet's dream—and part of a transcendent reality beyond himself. At last he becomes for the poet part of nature itself.

> In my mind's eye I seemed to see him pace
> About the weary moors continually,
> Wandering about alone and silently.

---

[16] Wordsworth's comment on this passage in the Preface of 1815—referring it to the work of the imagination alone—is instructive: "In these images, the conferring, the abstracting, and the modifying powers of the Imagination, immediately and mediately acting, are all brought into conjunction. The Stone is endowed with something of the power of life to approximate it to the Sea-beast; and the Sea-beast stripped of some of its vital qualities to assimilate it to the stone; which intermediate image is thus treated for the purpose of bringing the original image, that of the stone, to a nearer resemblance to the figure and condition of the aged Man; who is divested of so much of the indications of life and motion as to bring him to the point where the two objects unite and coalesce in just comparison." *Literary Criticism of William Wordsworth*, p. 149. My point is, of course, that this passage is not the work of imagination alone, but the work of fancy and imagination working in harmony.

Through the poet's vision of him, the old man has become consubstantial not only with the poet but with the world around and above him, bringing all nature, all time, and all eternity, it seems, to dwell in himself.

We have already said that poetry of the imagination is compounded of imagination and fancy, of symbol and metaphor. What is suggested by "Resolution and Independence" takes us a step further: that fancy at its best may set imagination in motion, that image and metaphor at their best, or most intense, move in the direction of symbol. Metaphor at its most intense aspires to the condition of symbol, as the poet strives to embrace more and more of reality. A poem of the imagination is necessarily, in Coleridgean terms, organic. It begins with a seed, a germ, which takes nourishment into itself and then proceeds to "put parts outside of parts." This germ may be a simple image or metaphor, but it can grow—as the leech-gatherer grows—to the dimensions of a symbol, complex and open and ultimately mysterious.

What, then, is the relationship between metaphor and symbol? Either—like the leech-gatherer—metaphor *becomes* symbol, or else—like the minor metaphors of the poem—it is caught up into, or subsumed under, a symbol larger than itself. Fancy may work alone, but at its best it is put at the service of the higher faculty, imagination. As we have heard Coleridge say before, "genius must have talent as its complement and implement, just as, in like manner, imagination must have fancy. In short, the higher intellectual powers can only act through a corresponding energy of the lower."[17]

The Prelude is, of course, Wordsworth's poem of the imagination *par excellence*. Yet it, too, is a poem worked out under the aegis of the imagination but with the constant concurrence of the fancy. If it is a poem of incomparable symbolic reference and resonance, it is at the same time a poem in which metaphor is used with incomparable skill.

---

[17] *TT*, I, 426 (August 17, 1833).

But, especially in a work of such length and such complexity, the ways in which symbol and metaphor interact may be expected to be many.

First, there are the clearly metaphorical passages, in *The Prelude* generally very skillfully crafted, that enlighten an experience for the moment with perfect clarity, but that do not go beyond this clarity of reference and vision. In Book III, for example, after expressing regret at the changes that have taken place at Cambridge and at his own missed opportunities there, Wordsworth continues:

> But peace to vain regrets! we see but darkly
> Even when we look behind us; and best things
> Are not so pure by nature that they needs
> Must keep to all, as fondly all believe,
> Their highest promise. If the Mariner
> When at reluctant distance he hath passed
> Some tempting Island, could but know the ills
> That must have fallen upon him, had he brought
> His bark to land upon the wished-for shore,
> Good cause would oft be his to thank the surf
> Whose white belt scared him thence, or wind that blew
> Inexorably adverse! for myself
> I grieve not; happy is the gowned Youth,
> Who only misses what I missed, who falls
> No lower than I fell.
>
> (III, 482–496)[18]

The metaphor is clear and graceful, the lesson sharply and tellingly drawn.

Very often, however, the case is different, and we find the same movement we saw in "Resolution and Independence"—metaphor moving in the direction of, and finally becoming, symbol. There is a charming and ultimately moving example earlier in the same book, in Wordsworth's description of St. John's College, in which a series of meta-

---

[18] All quotations from *The Prelude*, unless otherwise indicated, will be taken from *The Fourteen-Book Prelude*, ed. W. J. B. Owen, *The Cornell Wordsworth*, ed. Stephen Parrish (Ithaca, N.Y., 1985).

phors jostle each other fancifully before he turns to the more serious metaphors that express the depth of his feelings for Isaac Newton. Finally, metaphor is not enough to convey his sense of the mysterious presence of the solitary figure—and metaphor becomes, for a moment, symbol.

> The Evangelist St. John my Patron was;
> Three gothic Courts are his, and in the first
> Was my abiding-place, a nook obscure!
> Right underneath, the College Kitchens made
> A humming sound, less tuneable than bees,
> But hardly less industrious; with shrill notes
> Of sharp command and scolding intermixed.
> Near me hung Trinity's loquacious Clock,
> Who never let the quarters, night or day,
> Slip by him unproclaimed, and told the hours
> Twice over, with a male and female voice.
> Her pealing Organ was my neighbour too;
> And from my pillow, looking forth by light
> Of moon or favoring stars, I could behold
> The Antechapel, where the Statue stood
> Of Newton, with his prism, and silent face:
> The marble index of a Mind for ever
> Voyaging through strange seas of Thought, alone.
> (III, 46–63)

At the end, the image remains—the statue—and the metaphor remains—the "marble index of a mind." Yet we are ultimately in the realm of symbol, "Voyaging through strange seas of Thought, alone." There is the solitary figure, larger than ever he was in life, mysterious in his power, eternal, alone. No mere metaphor could contain this haunting vision.

That this movement from metaphor to symbol was in some degree a conscious process with Wordsworth becomes clear if we compare the last few lines of this passage with the version of 1805. There he had written:

> And, from my Bed-room, I in moonlight nights
> Could see, right opposite, a few yards off,
> The Antechapel, where the Statue stood

Of Newton, with his Prism and silent Face.
(III, 56–59; 1805 version)[19]

In the later version, Wordsworth has methodically removed literal elements ("right opposite, a few yards off"), introduced images of uncertainty or indefiniteness ("by light / Of moon or favouring stars"), and added the elements of mystery, solitude, and eternity ("The marble index of a mind for ever / Voyaging through strange seas of Thought, alone"). What he has done is deliberately to force metaphor in the direction of symbol—the symbol of the solitary adventurer on an eminence, which will become thematically more and more important throughout *The Prelude*, orchestrating to the final climactic vision on Mount Snowdon.

A more complex example of a passage in which metaphor becomes symbol is the boat-stealing episode in Book I of *The Prelude*. It begins with simple imagery (the willow tree, the rocky cove) and modest metaphor (the echoes are voices, the circles of light melt, the ridge above is an "elfin pinnace," the boat "went heaving through the water like a swan"). But as the "huge peak, black and huge" rears up from behind the ridge above, the scene darkens, the mood changes. There is a sudden clutch of the heart as the huge peak is seen to be alive, "as if with voluntary power instinct." Where there had been the peace of the "silent lake," edged with the boyish adventure of "an act of stealth and troubled pleasure," there is now only fear. It is a fear that grows, becomes deeper and more intense, as the metaphor of the living mountain becomes more intense and more mysterious, reaching even to the stars.

> I struck, and struck again,
> And, growing still in stature, the grim Shape
> Towered up between me and the stars, and still,
> For so it seemed, with purpose of its own
> And measured motion, like a living Thing
> Strode after me.
> (I, 380–385)

---

[19] *The Thirteenth-Book Prelude*, ed. Mark L. Reed, in *The Cornell Wordsworth*, ed. Stephen Parrish (Ithaca, N.Y., 1991).

Even after the boy's return "with trembling oars," the figure is not complete. What had begun as a mountain peak "instinct" with life and will had grown beyond itself—or drawn things into itself—had towered up to the stars and brought down news of things beyond, of "unknown modes of being," of "huge and mighty forms, that do not live like living men."

> but after I had seen
> That spectacle, for many days, my brain
> Worked with a dim and undetermined sense
> Of unknown modes of being; o'er my thoughts
> There hung a darkness, call it solitude
> Or blank desertion. No familiar Shapes
> Remained, no pleasant images of trees,
> Of sea or Sky, no colours of green fields,
> But huge and mighty Forms, that do not live
> Like living men, moved slowly through the mind
> By day, and were a trouble to my dreams.
>
> (I, 390–400)

We have moved from the world of metaphor, the world of "familiar shapes," into a world of symbol. There is no lesson to be drawn, only a sense of mystery—of an experience that can never be fully expressed, perhaps because the experience itself is never finished.

Another passage, far different in outcome, makes an interesting parallel to this. It is the passage in Book VI immediately following the poet's stunned discovery that he has crossed the Alps. With his companions he had followed "along the Simplon's steep and rugged road." Left for a time by their guide, two of the travelers made their way upward, full of "hopes that pointed to the clouds." Fearful of being lost, they soon descended, only to learn from a passing peasant that, all unknown to them, they had crossed the Alps. They still had "hopes that pointed to the clouds," yet these hopes had already been fulfilled—but without the ecstasy, the lifting of the heart, that had been anticipated. The sense of let-down, of anticlimax, is almost palpable.

Of even greater interest is the experience that follows.

The poet begins to reflect metaphorically on the experience he has just undergone. First, his imagination

> rose from the Mind's abyss
> Like an unfathered vapour that enwraps
> At once some lonely Traveller.
>
> (VI, 595–597)

The poet is now the lonely traveler, and there is a lesson for him in this experience. To his "conscious soul" he can say of the experience: "I recognise thy glory." But what of the unconscious self that still has "hopes that point to the clouds," that longs for the moment of vision? Its answer is, metaphorically, that it always has within itself "our being's heart and home," that it is at home when it has hope itself—

> hope that can never die,
> Effort, and expectation, and desire,
> And something evermore about to be.
>
> (VI, 607–609)

For a moment the metaphor changes to a military figure, expressing the same realization that fulfillment is not in the achievement but in the striving.

> Under such banners militant the Soul
> Seeks for no trophies, struggles for no spoils,
> That may attest her prowess, blest in thoughts
> That are their own perfection and reward.
>
> (VI, 610–613)

The beatitude that comes from such striving is

> like the mighty flood of Nile
> Poured from his fount of Abyssinian clouds
> To fertilize the whole Egyptian plain.
>
> (VI, 615–617)

So much for the poet's *reflection*, his metaphoric articulation of what he can *understand* about his feelings and their meaning. He has told us of them, clearly and movingly, but we have not *experienced* them. There is more to come. The melancholy has passed—through the moments of careful reflection—and the downward journey continues. The pace, brisk at first, begins to slow. As the journey slows, impressions begin to pour in upon the poet from the wild scene around him. As these impressions grow wilder and more intense, we no longer are spectators but are drawn ourselves into the savage scene. The very intensity of the telling, with the dynamic forward movement of the imagery itself, betrays that this is no longer a reflection on a past experience but a re-creation of the experience itself. We see and feel it all for ourselves:

> The immeasurable height
> Of woods decaying, never to be decayed,
> The stationary blasts of waterfalls,
> And in the narrow rent at every turn
> Winds thwarting winds, bewildered and forlorn,
> The torrents shooting from the clear blue sky,
> The rocks that muttered close upon our ears,
> Black drizzling crags that spake by the way-side
> As if a voice were in them, the sick sight
> And giddy prospect of the raving stream,
> The unfettered clouds, and region of the Heavens,
> Tumult and peace, the darkness and the light.
>   (VI, 625–636)

What is this experience? It is surely an experience of contradiction: the dying yet eternal woods; the moving yet stationary waterfall; the wild torrents seeming to pour forth from a peaceful sky—tumult and peace, darkness and light. Yet at the same time it is an experience of oneness, for all these struggling opposites

> Were all like workings of one mind, the features
> Of the same face, blossoms upon one tree,
> Characters of the great Apocalypse,
> The types and symbols of Eternity,
> Of first and last, and midst, and without end.
>   (VI, 637–641)

There is metaphor here once again in this final passage—one mind, one face, one tree—but quite different from the metaphors of the earlier "reflection." These are metaphors in the service of a larger vision—what I would call "grop-ing" metaphors, which try to express fragments of a vision they cannot contain. The properly symbolic vision during this experience of the descent is, once again, a vision of a mystery. It is one of the great human mysteries, or perhaps it is a composite of many mysteries—the relationship be-tween the One and the Many, the struggle of good and evil, the "reconciliation of opposites" (to use the Coleridgean phrase), the struggle between sadness and peace in the soul of the human person. One cannot say it is a vision of this or that; it is a vision of mystery.

This is not to say that this vision cannot bring peace. It can bring peace—in spite of all its tensions and ambigu-ities—because it is not merely a *vision* of mystery. One senses that, in experiencing this vision, and in re-creating it, the poet can now *accept* the fact of mystery. For this is one of the many functions of symbol, not only to help us see, but also to open us to the acceptance of mystery. Not only does symbol allow us to see the complexity of human expe-rience, but at the same time it holds this complexity in unity—the kind of emotional oneness that we can accept as somehow meaningful. Symbol does not explain mystery, but it helps us to live with it—even to live with it joyfully. It orders chaos, not conceptually but mythically.

Other examples abound of this working together of meta-phor and symbol, and of metaphor growing into symbol. There is the dream of the Arab (V, 50–141), in which the stone and the shell carried by the Arab are transmuted by the poet's imagination—without ceasing to be a stone and a shell—into two books, Euclid's *Elements* and (probably) the Koran. The significance of the emblems grows: the stone—"the One that held acquaintance with the stars"— encompassing "Reason, undisturbed by space or time"; the shell, for all its harmony, foretelling "destruction to the Children of the Earth," yet having divine power to "exhila-rate the Spirit, and to soothe, / Through every clime, the heart of human kind." The movement throughout is not from obscurity to clarity, but from clarity to complexity, as the meaning of the emblems expands in the poet's imagination. Even the figure of the Arab changes, becoming the figure of Don Quixote.

> And now
> He to my fancy had become the Knight
> Whose tale Cervantes tells; yet not the Knight,
> But was an Arab of the desert, too,
> Of these was neither, and was both at once.
>
> (V, 122–126)

But this Arab Quixote changes in his demeanor as well, from a masterful figure who can pontificate for the dreamer "with calm look," to a disturbed figure who sees in the wilderness behind him "the waters of the deep / Gathering upon us," riding off in fear

> o'er the illimitable Waste
> With the fleet waters of a drowning world
> In chase of him.
>
> (V, 137–139)

It is no wonder the poet "waked in terror" at a vision of such enormity and of such mystery.

One might instance, too, the poet's meeting with the wandering soldier (IV, 370–469)—so reminiscent of the old leech-gatherer—who seems to gather up in himself the whole world of the suffering poor, the world of war, sickness, hunger, and friendlessness—and who at the end, as David Perkins remarks, "fades into the context of nature."[20] Or one might turn to the great, tumultuous scene of Bartholomew Fair (VII, 675–772), beginning with a riot of humanity in its most bizarre forms—a deeply particularized scene—then moving out in imagination (the soul acting like the sea, which "propels from Zone to Zone / Its currents, magnifies its Shoals of life / Beyond all compass") to embrace the whole broad world of humanity. In all this enormous complexity, and without losing a sense of the

---

[20] *The Quest for Permanence: The Symbolism of Wordsworth, Shelley, and Keats* (Cambridge, Mass., 1959), p. 17.

complexity, the poet finds harmony, "the Spirit of Nature."
Or, finally, one might turn to the last great epiphany of *The
Prelude*, the ascent of Mount Snowdon (XIV, 1–129), in
which the splendid metaphor of the sea—"a silent sea of
hoary mist"—expands into a symbolic vision that includes
earth, sea and sky, the dark abyss, the human mind, the
transcendent Deity, whatever was and is and shall be, "till
Time shall be no more."

In addition to the passages in *The Prelude* that are clearly
metaphorical alone and those in which metaphor grows into
symbol, there are passages in which metaphor and symbol
interact in a somewhat different way. I am thinking particularly of passages in which both metaphor and symbol are
present, but remain distinct from each other in their interaction.

There is a deceptively simple-looking passage in Book IV
that becomes more complex the longer one ponders it—and
yet one remains convinced that it is at bottom somehow
relatively simple.

> As one who hangs down-bending from the side
> Of a slow-moving boat, upon the breast
> Of a still water, solacing himself
> With such discoveries as his eye can make,
> Beneath him, in the bottom of the deep,
> Sees many beauteous sights, weeds, fishes, flowers,
> Grots, pebbles, roots of trees, and fancies more;
> Yet often is perplexed, and cannot part
> The shadow from the substance, rocks and sky,
> Mountains and clouds reflected in the depth
> Of the clear flood, from things which there abide
> In their true Dwelling: now is crossed by gleam
> Of his own image, by a sun-beam now,
> And wavering motions, sent he knows not whence,
> Impediments that make his task more sweet—
> Such pleasant office have we long pursued,
> Incumbent o'er the surface of past time,
> With like success, nor often have appeared
> Shapes fairer, or less doubtfully discerned

Than these to which the Tale, indulgent Friend!
Would now direct thy notice.

(IV, 256–276)

The opening "as" signals that a simile is to begin. But it is not long before the multiplication of "beauteous sights"—soon mingled with a perplexing of the senses—suggests that we have moved more deeply into the simile than metaphor alone can bear. Things become confused. The things of beauty become broader and broader in compass: to the weeds, fishes, and flowers one expects to find beneath the water are added rocks and sky, mountains and clouds from above, the viewer's self, and finally "wavering motions, sent he knows not whence." All this has become an essentially symbolic vision, holding within itself a reach of reality no mere metaphor could hold, including unseen and unknown transcendent realities sent "he knows not whence." Yet this vision remains firmly contained within the structure of a simile, and a simile not yet even complete. For the referent of the simile is only now to be given: "Such pleasant offices have we long pursued, / Incumbent o'er the surface of past time." The memory of the poet is as beauteous, as perplexing, and as tenuous, as the vision in the water. Is this metaphor or symbol? Clearly, it is both. But at what point does the metaphor "become" symbol? Here, I suggest, the process is somewhat different: the one does not become the other, but they interact with each other without either of them losing its own identity.

A variation of this process is found in the description of the poet's entrance into London.

> On the roof
> Of an itinerant Vehicle I sate,
> With vulgar men about me, trivial forms
> Of houses, pavement, streets, of men and things;
> Mean shapes on every side: but at the instant
> When to myself it fairly might be said,
> The threshold now is overpassed,—(how strange

> That aught external to the living mind
> Should have such mighty sway! Yet so it was),
> A weight of ages did at once descend
> Upon my heart, no thought embodied, no
> Distinct remembrances; but weight and power,—
> Power growing under weight: alas! I feel
> That I am trifling: 'twas a moment's pause,—
> All that took place within me came and went
> As in a moment, yet with Time it dwells,
> And grateful memory, as a thing divine.
> (VIII, 543–559)

From the simple images of the scene itself, with hardly the intervention of metaphor—except for the very modest metaphors of the "threshold" and the "weight of ages"—he has moved into symbolic vision. The weight and power are from the indistinct past—the experience of them is "a thing divine"—yet they are bound up, in some unutterable way, with the scene before him: "how strange / That aught external to the living mind / Should have such mighty sway."

Something of this symbolic vision is now expressed, or at least the poet tries to express it, in the metaphor which follows, of the traveler "who from the open day / Hath passed with torches into some huge cave" (VIII, 560–561). But even as the metaphor begins—the "huge cave" will be the "vast metropolis" of London—the vision moves beyond the "fixities and definites" of metaphor to the indistinctness and complexity of symbol.

> He looks around and sees the Vault
> Widening on all sides; sees, or thinks he sees,
> Erelong the massy roof above his head,
> That instantly unsettles and recedes,—
> Substance and shadow, light and darkness, all
> Commingled, making up a Canopy
> Of shapes and forms, and tendencies to shape
> That shift and vanish, change and interchange
> Like Spectres, ferment silent and sublime!
> (VIII, 564–572)

Yet this is all contained within the overarching structure of a simple metaphor—the city seen as a cave—the metaphor embracing the symbol, but neither one absorbing or subsuming the other.

The movement of the experience has been complex, but the expression of it is perfect: the movement from simple image to complex symbol (the entry into London and the falling of the "weight of ages") is followed by a parallel metaphoric expression of the experience (the entry into the cave), containing the symbolic vision (the vision in the cave). Here, as in the vision from the side of the boat, the metaphoric and symbolic elements remain clearly distinct from each other, and yet they interact with great power. It is yet another expression of Coleridge's ideal: the fancy placed at the service of the imagination.

In Wordsworth's poetry we are indeed led into the poet's vision of mystery. The vehicles of his leading are many: intellect and will and memory, imagination and fancy, image and metaphor and symbol. All, in the view of both Coleridge and Wordsworth, are ultimately under the aegis of the imagination. The rest all serve—when imagination is working at its highest pitch—to create the symbolic world where the deepest encounter can take place. It is the encounter of the poet with his own deepest self, with the world of nature and of humankind, with the transcendent reality we call God. It is the encounter of the reader, too—through encounter with the poet and his poem—with all of these.

We have said that this encounter is with a world of mystery, and so it is. It is the special character of symbol that it is able to usher us into this world without taking away the mystery. Symbol reveals the deepest mysteries of human life, but respects their ultimate resistance to revelation. Symbol leaves the mysteries as it finds them—awesome, compelling, radiant with darkness and with light.

5

The Poetry of Encounter:
Coleridge

IT WOULD BE something less than justice to Coleridge to exemplify his idea of symbol solely from the poetry of Wordsworth. Wordsworth's poetry has been given priority, because it is from his work that Coleridge himself exemplifies his theory. Wordsworth is always, for Coleridge, the symbolic poet *par excellence*.

But it is more than mere courtesy that demands that we now turn to the poetry of Coleridge himself. First of all, a strong case can be made that it is Coleridge, not Wordsworth, who is the true originator. The original version of "The Eolian Harp" was written, after all, in 1795, the same year in which Wordsworth completed that very eighteenth-century poem, "Lines Left upon a Seat in a Yew-tree," and three years before "A Night-Piece" and "Tintern Abbey"—and "This Lime-tree Bower my Prison" was written in 1797. At least, we must concede the cogency of what Thomas McFarland has called the "symbiosis" of Coleridge and Wordsworth in their poetic development.[1] At the very least, one must take into account the extraordinary interplay of imaginations during the *annus mirabilis* at Nether Stowey and Alfoxden.

Secondly, there is the matter of the difference of Coleridge's style from that of Wordsworth. However much the "Conversation Poems" may turn out to be like Wordsworth's in their symbolic import, the "poems of the supernatural" open up other considerations about symbol that we must not ignore.

---

[1] "The Symbiosis of Coleridge and Wordsworth," *Studies in Romanticism*, 11 (1972), 263–303.

We begin with "The Eolian Harp," not because it is a perfect example of the poetry of symbolic encounter—it is, admittedly, something short of perfection in both conception and execution—but because its "one Life" passage stands so much at the center of Coleridge's poetic vision. We may not agree with Coleridge's own assessment of it as "the most perfect poem I ever wrote,"[2] but its importance cannot be overlooked.

The poem begins with the simplest of imagery: the cottage, the jasmine, the broad-leaved myrtle. It begins, too, by making these images what we have called the most modest of metaphors—emblems—"meet emblems they of Innocence and Love."[3] There is another emblem, "the star of eve / Serenely brilliant"—"such would Wisdom be"—and the more ambitious metaphor of the Lute, the "Eolian Harp" itself. But the more important movement of the poem is not a movement from image to image, from metaphor to metaphor, but a movement into a greater intensity. The first nine lines evoke, very noticeably, images of sight: the flowers, the clouds, the evening star. After a moment's appeal to the sense of smell—"how exquisite the scents / Snatch'd from yon bean-field"—the poet turns to images of sound. The world is hushed, the murmur of the sea "tells us of silence." Into that silence comes the sound of the wind-harp, beginning softly at the casement where the poet sits, growing louder as the breeze increases—"and now, its strings / Boldlier swept"—and at the same time moving outward in imagination as it becomes

> Such a soft floating witchery of sound
> As twilight Elfins make, when they at eve
> Voyage on gentle gales from Fairy-Land,
> Where Melodies round honey-dropping flowers,

[2] Cited by James Dykes Campbell, ed., *The Poetical Works of Samuel Taylor Coleridge* (London, 1893), p. 578.

[3] The text used for Coleridge's poems will be that of *The Complete Poetical Works of Samuel Taylor Coleridge*, ed. Ernest Hartley Coleridge (Oxford, 1912).

> Footless and wild, like birds of Paradise,
> Nor pause, nor perch, hovering on untam'd wing!

The poet has been released for the moment, it seems: he, too, is "footless and wild," he too "hover[s] on untam'd wing." In this momentary freedom there is a new intensity of feeling, joined with a mingling of the senses. Sight and sound are no longer separate, nor is he separate from the evening-world he has entered for the moment. In this moment of synaesthetic experience, there is a fusion not only of senses but also of life and being itself.

> O! the one Life within us and abroad,
> Which meets all motion and becomes its soul,
> A light in sound, a sound-like power in light,
> Rhythm in all thought, and joyance every where—
> Methinks, it should have been impossible
> Not to love all things in a world so fill'd.[4]

As M. H. Abrams says, in these lines "the poet breaks through sensation into vision, in which the phenomenal aspects of the landscape, its colors, music, and odors, are intuited as products and indices of the first manifestations of the creative Word, gravitation and light, in whose multiform unions all nature and life consist."[5] It is a moment of symbolic vision—one yet many, intensely personal yet universal, deeply mysterious.

The noon-day vision that follows the vision at evening is actually a reprise of the first experience, less successful, it must be confessed, not only because it is a reprise but also because the passage to the symbolic moment ("And what if all of animated nature / Be but organic Harps") is too abrupt, more a reflection than a shared experience.

As Sara's "mild reproof" brings the poet back from these "shapings of the unregenerate mind," we are brought back

---

[4] It should be noted that these lines were first added in the version published in *Sibylline Leaves* in 1817.

[5] "Coleridge's 'A Light in Sound': Science, Metascience, and Poetic Imagination," *Proceedings of the American Philosophical Society*, 116 (1972), 474–475.

once more to the metaphorical mode: these "shapings," the "bubbles that glitter," "Philosophy's aye-babbling spring." The poet "returns" to reflect on his own sinfulness and to thank God for the gifts of his simple cottage life with Sara.

Commonly, the "return" in a Coleridgean Conversation Poem is a return with new insight derived from the symbolic vision. The problem with "The Eolian Harp" is that one feels a gap, a fracture, between the almost mystical vision and the return, between the experience and its aftermath. But whether or not the poem is in the end, as has been so often suggested, a rejection of his vision in the name of what he takes to be Christian orthodoxy, there remains the symbolic vision itself. He has begun with the commonplace facts of a quiet moment of happiness: himself, his new wife,[6] their cottage, the flowers, the evening star, a wind-harp set in the casement. The wind sets in motion, though, not merely the harp but the poet's imagination as well, and we are carried in the second movement into a fantasy-world, further and further, it seems, from the actual world of their quiet evening together. In fact, however, the poet soon finds that this imaginative leap has carried him not away from reality but into a deeper awareness of the oneness of all things, whether present to him or not. He has come close to the heart of a deeper mystery of union than even that of this peaceful life together. As Ronald Wendling has said: ". . . the lute's music, previously associated with her 'sweet upbraiding,' is now the product of the union between breeze and lute, himself and Sara, creative imagination and the external nature it impregnates, the world 'within us' and the world 'abroad.' This 'child' of the poet is, of course, the symbol, fathered by the dissolving, diffusing, dissipating power of imagination as it informs the receptive materials of ordinary human experience."[7]

---

[6] It is unclear whether the original version of the poem dates from before or after Coleridge's marriage to Sara Fricker in October 1795, but imaginatively the setting is clear.

[7] "Coleridge and the Consistency of 'The Eolian Harp'," *Studies in Romanticism*, 8 (1968), 33.

The metaphor of birth is an especially apt one, since it is the one Coleridge himself so often uses: the imagination is "that reconciling and mediatory power, which . . . gives birth to a system of symbols."[8] This birth involves a passage from metaphor to symbol, from the working of fancy to the working of imagination. As Wendling puts it: "Coleridge himself first introduces the breeze, the lute and its music as the vehicles of a rather mechanical set of comparisons. . . . But in the 'one Life' passage, his imagination takes hold of these products of fancy and generates in them a set of symbols."[9] The materials to be held in a single vision have become so broad, so disparate, even so paradoxical, that they cannot be held in balance except by a symbol, which can embrace without confining, which can hold in a single "field of force" whatever is drawn within its orbit.

As further examples of the symbolic vision of the Conversation Poems, it is tempting to turn to "This Lime-tree Bower my Prison" or "Dejection: An Ode." They exemplify perfectly the kind of interplay of metaphor and symbol we have been talking about, advancing to a moment of symbolic vision—or, in the case of "Dejection," to several such moments—of great intensity and beauty. However, in light of everything we have already said—and granted Coleridge's terminology and point of view—their symbolic character will be perfectly evident. A more interesting example, because it is not quite so evident and because its movement is rather different from "The Eolian Harp," is "The Nightingale."

"The Nightingale" begins, like all the Conversation Poems, quietly. It is evening, and the poet's fancy responds to the silent scene before him: the mossy bridge, the silent glimmer of the stream beneath, the dim stars above. It is, clearly, the work of fancy, but yielding beauty in no small measure. Thinking of the dimness of the stars, the poet recalls the rain this dimness portends, and his fancy suggests:

---

[8] *LS*, p. 29.
[9] Wendling, p. 33.

> let us think upon the vernal showers
> That gladden the green earth, and we shall find
> A pleasure in the dimness of the stars.

Then comes the sound of the nightingale, and its song suggests to the poet's fancy Milton's phrase from "Il Penseroso," "most musical, most melancholy." Here begins what can only be called a flight of fancy—the poet's thought that only one who was filled with woe could hear the song of the nightingale and call it anything but joyful. It was some "poor wretch" who

> filled all things with himself,
> And made all gentle sounds tell back the tale
> Of his own sorrow.

Poets ever after have taken up the same "conceit." Thus far, Coleridge's own response to the song has been a fanciful conceit of his own, just as the poem itself so far has been the work of his fancy, light and charming, personally almost unengaged.

But now what the poet of the past has done with the conceit of the nightingale is contrasted with what the poet should be doing. What he should be doing is not using the "fixities and definites" of the world around him (here, the song of the nightingale) as counters in a fanciful game of his own creation, but opening himself up to the whole world of things and values around him—not so much singling out and detaching as embracing and allowing himself to be embraced.

> he had better far have stretched his limbs
> Beside a brook in mossy forest-dell,
> By sun or moon-light, to the influxes
> Of shapes and sounds and shifting elements
> Surrendering his whole spirit, of his song
> And of his fame forgetful! so his fame
> Should share in Nature's immortality,
> A venerable thing! and so his song
> Should make all Nature lovelier, and itself
> Be loved like Nature!

This is not yet, I think, a symbolic vision. It is, rather, fancy enunciating a need for something beyond itself, a symbolic imperative. It is this symbolic imperative that becomes a basis for the rest of the poem.

For poets who rely on fancy alone, " 'twill not be so"— the symbolic imperative will not be felt. However, the poet and his friends (William and Dorothy Wordsworth) "have learnt / A different lore." They have learned that "Nature's sweet voices," including that of the nightingale, are "always full of love / And joyance." But not only has the poet learned, I suggest, that the nightingale's song is joyous but—as is evidenced by the rest of the poem, the aftermath of this reflection—he has also learned to *be* like the nightingale, who can

> utter forth
> His love-chant, and disburthen his full soul
> Of all its music!

The nightingale—part of Nature and in tune with Nature— sings freely, not by convention. He "disburthen[s] his full soul / Of all its music!" The poet, too, can sing freely. By opening himself to the reality around him, by "surrendering his whole spirit" to the "shapes and sounds and shifting elements" of the world, he too can "disburthen his full soul / Of all its music."

So this is what the poet now does: he sings his song. This is the answer to the problem readers have occasionally had with this part of the poem, those who have felt the poem begins to wander from its subject, with the introduction of the abortive, vaguely medieval tale of the castle and the "gentle Maid."[10] What we have is actually a song within a song, and the organic link between them is the song of the nightingales.

The poet's new song, his own musical "disburthening," begins with a narrative, a narrative that is never ended, but whose setting grows in intensity to the point of symbolic

---

[10] See George Watson, *Coleridge the Poet* (London, 1966), pp. 72–73.

vision. The narrative is, of course, merely suggested, by the castle, the great lord, the wild grove. It is used only to set the new song in motion. The song very shortly belongs to the nightingales, whose music fills the wood and thicket and the whole wide grove, as "they answer and provoke each other's song." Their song is soon the unifying force of the scene, especially

> one low piping sound more sweet than all—
> Stirring the air with such a harmony,
> That should you close your eyes, you might almost
> Forget it was not day!

This brief moment of harmony is not of sound alone, for it is accompanied by the sight of the nightingales themselves perched on moonlit bushes, their "bright, bright eyes" glistening in the moonlight, while in the shadow the glow-worms give off their softer light.

This moment of vision—symbolic in its unity and its suggestiveness—is only the prelude to a fuller vision yet to come. The movement advances with a momentary return to the narrative mode:

> A most gentle Maid,
> Who dwelleth in her hospitable home
> Hard by the castle . . .
> Glides through the pathways.

Again, this is only the framework for a deeper movement: it is the Maid who hears again the sound of the nightingales, and, significantly, she is "like a Lady vowed and dedicate / To something more than Nature in the grove." The vision toward which we are moving is beyond mere Nature; there is "something more than Nature in the grove." Instead of, as before, a harmony of sounds, here there is first "a pause of silence," at the same moment as the moon is "lost behind a cloud." It is a silence that is "heard," a portentous silence, and when the moon emerges there is a burst of harmony. This burst of harmony is the symbolic moment toward which the poem has been moving, and it quickly grows in

intensity of feeling, almost invoking, it seems, the memory
of "The Eolian Harp" and its vision of oneness.

> she knows all their notes,
> That gentle Maid! and oft, a moment's space,
> What time the moon was lost behind a cloud,
> Hath heard a pause of silence; till the moon
> Emerging, hath awakened earth and sky
> With one sensation, and those wakeful birds
> Have all burst forth in choral minstrelsy,
> As if some sudden gale had swept at once
> A hundred airy harps!

The vision ends beautifully—and rather delightfully—with
a glimpse of the ecstasy of just one of this whole world of
nightingales, his song now in tune with the breeze and the
whole world of earth and sky:

> And she hath watched
> Many a nightingale perch giddily
> On blossomy twig still swinging from the breeze,
> And to that motion tune his wanton song
> Like tipsy Joy that reels with tossing head.

As the vision ends, there is a graceful return from the
single ecstatic nightingale of the vision to the original nightingale of the poem: "Farewell, O Warbler! til tomorrow
eve." There is a graceful return, too, to the friends with
whom he had paused on the mossy bridge. Finally, there is
the typically Coleridgean blessing, part of the fruit of his
vision. Here it is the blessing of his child, that he may grow
into a share in this vision, that he may know not only the
evening-star and the calming influence of the moon but also
the joy of the nightingale's song.

Clearly, there is a symbolic vision at the heart of this
poem, a vision of oneness, of mystery, of joy. What is "the
symbol" in this symbolic vision? Once again, it is not this
or that, though images and metaphors continually point to
this and that: the nightingale's love-chant, the glow-worm's
touch, the airy harps, tipsy Joy. The "symbol," if so it may
be called, is the whole experience of sound and motion—

ultimately of mysterious oneness—of earth and sky and all things everywhere, with the nightingale's song as its point of focus. The symbol is somehow *between* the metaphors, or, rather, around them, embracing them and giving them fuller life. As always, the symbol remains only describable, not definable.

Discussion of "The Rime of the Ancient Mariner" traditionally begins with Coleridge's famous conversation with that lady of "fine taste," Mrs. Barbauld. We shall be no breakers of tradition. Mrs. Barbauld had complained (as Coleridge reports the conversation in *Table Talk*) of the poem's want of a moral.[11] On the contrary, Coleridge had replied, "the only, or chief fault, if I may say so, was the obtrusion of the moral sentiment so openly on the reader as a principle or cause of action in a work of pure imagination." Is this to deny that the poem has "meaning," moral or otherwise? Surely not. Coleridge is no doubt referring to the Mariner's "moral" at the end of the poem ("He prayeth best, who loveth best . . .") intruding too obviously on the tale, with the danger of limiting its meaning in the reader's mind. We are back once again to Coleridge's distinction between allegory and symbol, between definable meaning and (virtually) indefinable meaning.

What is important about "The Ancient Mariner" in the context of our argument is that the poem poses one of the central problems raised by symbol and symbolic poetry: the problem of meaning. One of the areas of human and poetic concern articulated in the poem is precisely the problem of symbol, how the human mind articulates its experience of worlds that remain ultimately mysterious and impenetrable.

One of the best clues we have about all this is often ignored, the introductory motto to the poem—a somewhat doctored quotation from Thomas Burnet's *Archeologiae Philosophicae* (1692). It is commonly ignored, one may suppose, because it is in Latin, but, like the prose glosses

---

[11] *TT*, I, 272–273 (March 31, 1832). See also Coleridge's earlier remarks on the subject, *TT*, I, 149 (May 30, 1830).

added at the same time, it remains part of the text as Coleridge left it to us. For my own part, I find that both the motto and the glosses add immeasurably not only to the clarity of movement of the poem—no doubt the reason Coleridge added them for the version published in 1817—but also to its richness. The glosses were Coleridge's answer to the contemporary reader's difficulty in following the complex movement of the action; they do not remove the complexity, but they afford a pathway through it that will allow the reader to experience the mysteries through which the poem moves. The Latin motto, too, is meant to be a direction-signal, but of a different sort. If the glosses are road-signs, then the motto is a kind of general warning about the conditions of the road, the terrain, and the weather ahead.

> Facile credo, plures esse Naturas invisibiles quam visibiles in rerum universitate. Sed horum [*sic*] omnium familiam quis nobis enarrabit? et gradus et cognationes et discrimina et singulorum munera? Quid agunt? quae loca habitant? Harum rerum notitiam semper ambivit ingenium humanum, nunquam attigit. Juvat, interea, non diffiteor, quandoque in animo, tanquam in tabula, majoris et melioris mundi imaginem contemplari: ne mens assuefacta hodiernae vitae minutiis se contrahat nimis, et tota subsidat in pusillas cogitationes. Sed veritati interea invigilandum est, modusque servandus, ut certa ab incertis, diem a nocte, distinguamus.[12]

Essentially, as we enter this poem we are warned by Coleridge's motto not to expect overmuch clarity of vision. It is

---

[12] Translation: "I readily believe that there are more invisible than visible things in the universe. But who shall describe for us their families, their ranks, relationships, distinguishing features and functions? What do they do? Where do they live? The human mind has always circled about knowledge of these things, but never attained it. I do not doubt, however, that it is sometimes good to contemplate in the mind, as in a picture, the image of a greater and better world; otherwise the intellect, habituated to the petty things of daily life, may too much contract itself, and wholly sink down to trivial thoughts. But meanwhile we must be vigilant for truth and keep proportion, that we may distinguish the certain from the uncertain, day from night." The translation is from *English Romantic Writers*, ed. David Perkins (New York, 1967), p. 405.

a complex world, or worlds, we are entering, and it is full of mysteries. Nor are they mysteries we can ever expect fully to comprehend: "Harum rerum notitiam semper ambivit ingenium humanum, nunquam attigit." "Semper" and "nunquam" are strong words: always searching, never simply finding once for all. We are warned even before we start that this is a poem about worlds too vast to be fully conquered, about mysteries too deep to be encompassed by mere words—and yet about the need to try to conquer them, to encompass them—a poem, therefore, of symbolic weight and import.

In order to bring more sharply into focus the problem of symbolic meaning raised by "The Ancient Mariner," it will be helpful to turn to the studies of the poem by Robert Penn Warren and Humphry House. Taken together, they can shed light on the matter precisely because they disagree rather strongly on the symbolic meaning of the poem.

Robert Penn Warren's famous essay "A Poem of Pure Imagination: An Experiment in Reading"[13] begins with what is for some a suspect goal, "to establish that *The Ancient Mariner* does embody a statement, and to define the nature of that statement, the theme, as nearly as I can" (p. 201). As he puts it later in the essay: "If *The Ancient Mariner* has a meaning, what is that meaning?" (p. 212). It soon becomes clear, however, that the second formulation of his goal is perhaps the more accurate: it is more properly a search for meaning than a search for statement. For the search is conducted in the full light—reflected in the title of the essay—of Coleridge's idea of the imagination, which "brings the whole soul of man into activity," not merely his discursive powers. If there is "meaning" in the poem, it will not be merely discursive, but mediated by all our cognitive faculties, emotional as well as intellectual, instinctive as well as conscious.

First of all, in "The Ancient Mariner" Warren finds multiple meaning, even on the thematic level. "Any substantial

---

[13] *Selected Essays* (New York, 1958), pp. 198–305.

work will operate at more than one thematic level, and this is what makes it so difficult to define *the* theme of a profound creation; the root-idea will have many possible formulations, and many of them will appear, or be suggested, in the work" (p. 213). It should be evident, then, that when Warren goes on "to distinguish two basic themes, both of them very rich and provocative," he is undertaking no simple—to say nothing of simplistic—definition of the poem's unique meaning. For all its clarity of formulation, his "definition" itself remains "rich and suggestive."

Warren distinguishes two themes in the poem, one primary, the other secondary. He hastens to add that this does not imply a judgment of relative importance, but only that the first is "more obviously presented to us, is, as it were, at the threshold of the poem" (p. 214). The primary theme is "the theme of sacramental vision, or the theme of the 'One Life.' " The secondary theme is "the theme of the imagination." He then goes on to show the interrelationship, indeed the "symbolic fusion," of these two themes.

Approaching the primary theme, Warren first summarizes "the fable, in broadest and simplest terms," as "a story of crime and punishment and repentance and reconciliation": "The Mariner shoots the bird; suffers various pains, the greatest of which is loneliness and spiritual anguish; upon recognizing the beauty of the foul sea snakes, experiences a gush of love for them and is able to pray; is returned miraculously to his home port, where he discovers the joy of human communion in God, and utters the moral, 'He prayeth best who loveth best, etc.' We arrive at the notion of a universal charity . . . the sense of the 'One Life' in which all creation participates" (p. 222).

This mere retelling of the fable is not enough, because this is poetry of symbol, not of allegory. Symbol for Coleridge is "focal and massive," says Warren (p. 218). It "involves an idea (or ideas) as part of its potential, but it also involves the special complex of feelings associated with that idea, the attitude toward that idea. The symbol affirms the unity of mind in the welter of experience. . . . It represents a focus of being . . ." (p. 218). Besides being "focal and massive," symbol is "not arbitrary—not a mere sign—but contains within itself the appeal which makes it serviceable as a symbol" (p. 218). The symbol "has to participate in the unity of which it is representative. And this means that the symbol has a deeper relationship to the total structure of meaning than its mechanical place in plot, situation, or discourse" (p. 220).

The "fable," then—the killing of the albatross and its consequences—must be seen in the context of its whole symbolic setting. Its total setting must be kept in balance if we are to enter into the mystery of this supposedly wanton act. It is a setting of human pleasures and hungers, of human pieties and impieties, but it is also a setting of natural beauties and horrors, of supernatural revelations of stunning magnitude and haunting suggestiveness. The killing of the albatross is not apart from the other natural and human images of the poem or from those of its supernatural world. Symbolically they are one. Each image, each act, is part of a larger unity. What happens in one realm has consequences for everything else in the poem. By living through, with the Mariner, the consequences of his act—consequences in the world of nature, of men, and of the supernatural, consequences that are awesome and terrifying, beautiful and mysterious—we come to learn the meaning of one aspect of his crime and that of his fellow sailors: "They have violated the sacramental conception of the universe, by making man's convenience the measure of an act, by isolating him from Nature and the 'One Life' " (p. 232). Only by immersing ourselves in the central action in all its particularity—the criminal act with all its mysterious consequences—will we be able to sense, if not to articulate, its meaning.

However, the second of Warren's themes is demanded, he says, by lacunae left in the articulation of the first: "If in the poem one follows the obvious theme of the 'One Life' as presented by the Mariner's crime, punishment, and reconciliation, one is struck by the fact that large areas of the poem seem to be irrelevant to this business: for instance, the special atmosphere of the poem, and certain images which, because of the insistence with which they are presented, seem to be endowed with a special import" (p. 233).

In other words, the first theme does not account for the poem in its fullness; in particular, it does not account for the recurrence of certain images. Warren focuses especially on the imagery of light: sun and moon, stars, bright light and half-light, and a whole congeries of others. What emerges is the establishment in the poem of certain patterns of imagery, and "once the import of an image is established for our minds, that image cannot in its workings upon us elsewhere in the poem be disencumbered, whether or not we are consciously defining it" (p. 237). The patterns, or "symbolic clusters," are focused generally around the imagery of light, as, for example, early in the poem we have the association of "the creative wind, the friendly bird, the moonlight of imagination, all together in one symbolic cluster" (p. 239). As the poem develops, it becomes clear that there are certain symbols, notably the moon, that are generally beneficent; others, especially the sun, are usually malevolent; still others, like the wind, remain ambiguous— sometimes creative, sometimes destructive.

It is by such means as these, too, that the two themes—the sacramental and the aesthetic—are fused. "As soon as the cluster [the initial beneficent cluster centering in the moon] is established, the crime, with shocking suddenness, is announced. We have seen how the crime is to be read at the level of the primary theme. At the level of the secondary theme it is, of course, a crime against the imagination. Here, in the crime, the two themes are fused" (p. 239). There is the beneficent symbol of the moon, then the crime, then: "The sun now rose upon the right." It is as if, Warren says, the crime brings the sun in place of the beneficent moon (p. 240).

It is impossible to do justice in a short space to the richness and subtlety of Warren's long discussion of Coleridge's development of these two themes. What is important for us here, though, is that the two themes—for all the clar-

ity of Warren's articulation of them—remain richly suggestive, and that they are not separate, but "fused" (to use
Coleridge's word) by the energies of the poem. As Warren
says of the "final fusion of the imagination and the sacramental vision," we "may, as it were, take them to be aspects
of the same reality" (p. 248). The poem was written out of
the belief that "the moral concern and the aesthetic concern
are aspects of the same activity, the creative activity, and
that this activity is expressive of the whole mind." The
poem "is, in general, about the unity of mind and the final
unity of values, and in particular about poetry itself"
(p. 253). It is ultimately the beneficent light of imagination
that heals and reconciles, that brings all things, including
the sacramental universe, into harmony. Ultimately, the
still-haunted Mariner, wandering about the world to tell his
tale, is the poet himself. The moral imperative and the aesthetic imperative are not separate.

Humphry House, in his essay "The Ancient Mariner,"[14]
is more than a bit uncomfortable with Warren's reading of
the poem, particularly with the degree of specificity to
which Warren commits himself. House's problem is not
with the first theme; the sacramental theme of "One Life"
is broad enough to be compatible with the sin/redemption
movement that all modern critics have admitted to be at the
heart of the poem. The questions House asks, with some
urgency, focus on Warren's reading of the second theme:
"How far does it succeed in giving a coherent and convincing explanation of the miscellaneous detail in the difficult
parts of the poem? And in what sense does it establish that
there is a theme which *is* 'the theme of the imagination'?"
(p. 107). House's answers to both these questions are
strongly critical.

The difference between them turns, as House himself
points out, on the conception of symbol. "Mr. Warren," he
says, "seems in the last resort to be a precisionist" (p. 108).

---

[14] *Coleridge: The Clark Lectures, 1951–52* (London, 1953), pp. 84–
113.

"What seems to have happened," he goes on, "is that Mr. Warren, delighted by the relative coherence of the moon–bird–mist–wind cluster, has forced other items into congruence with it, by minimising differences in their character and in their emotional effects. But such forcing would not have been necessary if he had started out with a less rigid theory of symbolic reference" (p. 110). Warren moves, he contends, from "what is richly and variously suggestive into what is precise and technical," and as a result the "theme of the imagination" is "something narrower and more technical than the poem can carry" (p. 110). Warren defines, as we might otherwise put it, what is ultimately indefinable; he tends to translate symbol into allegory.

These are weighty charges indeed. Yet when we turn to House's own reading of the poem, we find him also defining—perhaps not so precisely, but defining all the same. House focuses strongly on the two very evident worlds of the poem, the world of the Mariner and the world of the Wedding-Guest. The recurring interruptions of the Mariner's tale by the Wedding-Guest are meant to underscore the differences between these two worlds. The spiritual odyssey of the Mariner takes place within both these worlds, and the poem about his experience deliberately brings them into sharp contrast. At bottom, it is a contrast "between two aspects of reality, and two potentialities of experience, the visible bodily world of human beings marrying and giving in marriage and an invisible world of spirits and the dead where quite a different system of values is to be learnt. The effect of the interruptions of the Wedding-Guest is to show how these two kinds of reality are always co-existent: the total effect of the poem is to show them interpenetrating" (p. 96).

In his flight from precision, House suggests that "if we accept the term 'symbol' we must allow symbols a freer, wider, less exact reference" (pp. 107–108). Yet we may ask whether there is not room, in reading the truly symbolic poem, for both the more and the less precise? Will there not always be greater and lesser degrees of clarity of reference?

It is true, of course—as House concludes—that "the emphasis is on the mystery and the richness of the mystery.
Through the development of the imagery we are gradually
led into the realisation that the values of 'the land of mist
and snow' are of the greatest possible concern, but that they
are indescribable" (p. 113). Yet is it true that they are *wholly*
indescribable? Were they so, there would be no poem. There
are, after all, the moments of vision: the icy beauty of the
polar regions, the vision of the water snakes, the apparitions
of the heavenly spirits, the lights and half-lights of a score
of other moments—all mysterious, to be sure, but not totally
"indescribable."

House makes much of one sentence from the Latin motto
of Burnet's with which our discussion began: "Harum
rerum notitiam semper ambivit ingenium humanum, nunquam attigit." It is true enough that we will never come to
an end of our pondering of the symbolic experience of this
poem. It is, as I. A. Richards says of the greatest myths,
"inexhaustible to meditation." But House does not take into
account the rest of Burnet's (and Coleridge's) injunction:
"Juvat, interea, non diffiteor, quandoque in animo, tanquam
in tabula, majoris et melioris mundi imaginem contemplari"
("I do not doubt, however, that it is sometimes good to contemplate in the mind, as in a picture, the images of a greater
and better world"). If it is true that we can never define the
meaning or meanings of the symbolic experience of "The
Ancient Mariner," or of any symbolic poem, to say that it
means uniquely this or that, it is also true that we must always try to articulate (as Robert Penn Warren does, as Humphry House does) what we can understand of it. To do this
is only to do what Coleridge himself strove to do: to articulate for us his own vision of mystery.

We need not choose between Warren and House, between
(to use House's terms) relative "precision" and relative "indefiniteness." As long as the precision does not descend to
"mere" allegory, as Warren's surely does not, and as long
as the indefiniteness does reach the point of articulate
speech, as House's triumphantly does, then both are work-

ing in the spirit of Coleridge. There is room for precision in the articulation of symbol, as long as it does not claim to be all. There is room for indefiniteness, as long as it does not abdicate the search for meaning. The Nicene definition of the consubstantiality of the Son with the Father does not deny the ultimate mystery of the Trinity, nor does the confession of the mystery negate the validity of the definition. As in "The Ancient Mariner," we articulate what we can, in faithfulness to the revelation (or the poem) set before us; the rest is mystery.

"The Ancient Mariner" is central to our consideration because it is about—at least among other things—the symbolic process itself. Perhaps Coleridge himself was only dimly aware of this at the time of its original composition. But it was the work of his, whether poetic or prose, over which he pondered longest and labored most. By 1817 he saw more deeply into the poem than ever before, and his addition of the glosses and especially of the motto from Burnet is his way of trying to bring into sharper focus what he was most deeply about. "The Ancient Mariner," the Latin quotation tells us, is the poet's attempt to represent symbolically what can never be fully represented—visible and invisible things and all their relationships, the "petty things of daily life" and "the image of a greater and better world," certain and uncertain, day and night, the vagaries of the human mind itself—a multiplicity of things, even a multiplicity of worlds. It can never be fully done, but the poet must try.

How can it be done at all? Only by symbol, which leaves the mystery intact even as it reveals a vision of unity. The poet discovers what the Mariner himself has discovered, that, in the words of Richard Haven, "the realist looks to experience, but in experience, the Mariner discovers, there is another dimension than time and space, a dimension in which the boundaries between subject and object, between *I* and *it* are not fixed but fluid."[15] We are once again in the

---

[15] *Patterns of Consciousness: An Essay on Coleridge* (Amherst, Mass., 1969), p. 20.

realm of transcendence and consubstantiality, of the communication between worlds, of the expression in symbols of
time and space of mysteries that are neither temporal nor
spatial. Coleridge's "Ancient Mariner" is surely about
meaning and the communication of meaning. The disparate
worlds must be brought together—the world of the Mariner
and the world of the Wedding-Guest, the world of the self
and the world outside, the immanent world of time and
space and the transcendent world of spiritual reality. They
must be brought within a single vision. This is the poet's
task—and his agony. Like the Mariner's, his tale will never
be fully and finally told; the symbol will never be enough.
But he must try.

What happens in the poem, for most of us, is what
happens in any truly symbolic poetry, any "poetry of encounter": we are drawn into the experience. Like the
Wedding-Guest, we are caught and held fast by the Mariner's
glittering eye. We are brought into what seems a dream but,
as in a dream, its experiences—of sin and redemption, of
alienation and communion, of darkness and light—become
startlingly real. As Richard Haven says, "we are made to
share the Mariner's experience to such a degree that we are
forced to acknowledge its reality, to realize that in form and
quality if not in circumstance, what happened to him may
happen to us. And one great achievement of the poem is that
it permits us, compels us, to contemplate these possibilities
of experience which our rational intelligence normally will
not let us admit" (p. 22). Through symbolic vision we are
brought to see, if not to comprehend, new worlds, new possibilities, new—and yet ancient—mysteries.

We have spoken much about "symbolic vision," so it is
perhaps appropriate that we turn at last to "Kubla Khan,"
which Coleridge subtitled "A Vision in a Dream."

Most modern critics have not taken very seriously (nor
need we) Coleridge's claim that the poem was composed
"in a profound sleep," and yet it is true that the poem does
have some of the qualities of a dream: exceptional clarity of
vision, more than ordinary preciseness of reference, joined

with strange, even bizarre, relationships between the things so sharply seen. What is perhaps more important is that it is "a vision." But what constitutes the vision? Should this be taken to refer only to the second part of the poem, the vision of the "damsel with a dulcimer"? Or is not the vision rather the dual vision of the whole poem—the first part ("In Xanadu did Kubla Khan") presented as a vision of a certain reality, the second ("A damsel with a dulcimer") as a vision of the ideal of this same reality. And does not this very duality tell us something about the nature of our theme, symbolic vision?

The vision of Xanadu itself is almost matter-of-fact in its portrayal of this exotic world. It is, to be sure, a vision of opposites: sunless and sun-drenched; garden and wilderness; savage and sacred; disciplined and wildly uncontrolled; raging river and lifeless ocean; a paradise, yet threatened by destruction. But for all the contrarieties, the vision is of a world that is somehow strangely one. This is precisely the "miracle," that the opposites are here reconciled: "It was a miracle of rare device, / A sunny pleasure-dome with caves of ice!"

The other part of the vision projects an ideal world, in which the reality of Kubla's world would owe its being to the poet's gift. It would be of his own making and, perhaps most important, would not be subject to destruction, as Kubla's creation is. It would be built "in air," that is, in the deathless words of the poet. It is the ancient and perennial theme of poets in all ages: "Exegi monumentum aere perennius." This vision too reconciles the same disparate realities, but the source of unity is inward, the poet's imagination.

Is not this, then, at least one of the truths the poem reveals about symbolic vision: that it has to do with both the real and the ideal, with a world that is objectively many and yet one, and a world that is made so by subjective envisioning? One might say that the two worlds are contrasted: the practical, actual world of the empire builder and the ideal world of the poet. Yet the poem, as symbol, is able to articulate more than mere contrast. If there is a complex oneness *within* each of these worlds—opposites held in balance— there is also a deep oneness *between* these two worlds. If they are objective and subjective, real and ideal, they are also ultimately one world. The second vision is only a deeper vision of the same reality.

Much has been written of "Alph, the sacred river." Is it the river of life or the river of the imagination? Symbolically, it should not be said to be simply one or the other. In the first part of the poem, it is of course—whatever else it may be—a river of life, passing through the complexities of human experience. In the second vision, we must not forget that the river is still present, though only by implication, just as the whole of Kubla's world is present. It is part of what the poet would build, part of his vision. And here— whatever else it may be—it is the river of imagination, for that is the energic force of the poet's vision. These rivers are not totally apart from each other; they are ultimately consubstantial with each other, just as these two worlds— the actual and the ideal—are consubstantial, just as life and poetry are consubstantial. There is one river, one world, one vision, and "one Life within us and abroad."

What, then, is a symbolic vision? At bottom it is no different from the vision humankind has always had, a vision of the real world, with all its complexities, set side by side with an ideal world, no less complex but (one always hopes) without the constant threat of destruction. What is new is that both these worlds can be contained within a single eye, a single vision. Or, rather, perhaps it is that vision and dream are no longer separate, or that imagination sees—in a single vision—beyond the merely actual and the merely objective, and beyond the "merely metaphorical."

All truly symbolic poetry is in some sense visionary poetry—the word of a seer, a dreamer of dreams, but not the seer who is merely an onlooker, who does not yield in faith and trust to the reality of the dream. Coleridge and Wordsworth dream, and yet their dreams are real. Perhaps ultimately this was their greatest achievement, to restore the prophet's trust in the vision, the dreamer's faith in the dream.

> Beware, beware!
> His flashing eyes, his floating hair!
> Weave a circle round him thrice
> And close your eyes with holy dread,
> For he on honey-dew hath fed,
> And drunk the milk of Paradise.

6

The Scriptural Imagination

TURNING FROM COLERIDGE'S POETRY to his views on "scriptural imagination" may seem at first blush rather a far reach, but this chapter is in fact as much about Coleridge's reading of the poetry of the scriptures as about theory. In a sense, it is yet another application of his theory of symbol to poetic practice, in this case that of the inspired authors of Scripture.

Although Coleridge often throughout his life used scriptural examples of poetic thought and practice, the privileged source is his remarkable essay of 1816, *The Statesman's Manual.*[1] While we have referred frequently to this seminal work already, its importance demands that we look at it more closely and on its own terms.

In spite of the fact that we have been reading *The Statesman's Manual* for over 175 years now, I venture to say that in modern times we have hardly looked very seriously at the *text*. For one reason and another—mainly because of their close attention to the human faculties—we have tended to pay much more attention to Coleridge's appendices, on Reason and Understanding, Conscience and Will, Ideas, and Symbol. Perhaps the fault is not wholly ours, however, since Coleridge himself has so swollen the appendices that they

---

[1] In *Coleridge and the Inspired Word* (Kingston, 1985), chap. 3, Anthony John Harding mines skillfully and sensitively the other important source for Coleridge's views on Scripture, the "Letters on the Inspiration of the Scriptures," published posthumously as *Confessions of an Inquiring Spirit* (1840) by his nephew Henry Nelson Coleridge. Harding's chapter 2, on the German *Naturphilosophie* in relation to Coleridge's theory of imagination, is also illuminating, particularly in his strong and cogent argument against a pantheistic view of Coleridge (pp. 65–71). On Coleridge's view of Scripture, especially as enunciated in *Confessions of an Inquiring Spirit*, see also Barth, *Coleridge and Christian Doctrine*, chap. 3.

threaten to overwhelm the text: in R. J. White's splendid edition in the *Collected Coleridge*, the text runs for forty-seven pages, the appendices for fifty. I should like to suggest, however, that the heart of the work may be, after all, in the text itself—in what Coleridge says, expressly or by implication, about the imagination as it is manifested in the Bible, "The Best Guide to Political Skill and Foresight."

Very early in *The Statesman's Manual*, Coleridge calls his contemporaries to look beyond the so-called miraculous element of the Bible. "In the infancy of the world," he argues, "signs and wonders were requisite in order to startle and break down that superstition, idolatrous in itself and the source of all other idolatry, which tempts the natural man to seek the true cause and origin of public calamities in outward circumstances, persons and incidents."[2] For the function of the biblical miracles was precisely to lead beyond themselves, to point to the "principles" (p. 10) from which they took their origin. As Coleridge says, "with each miracle worked there was a truth revealed, which thence forward was to act as its substitute" (p. 9). Miracles were to be replaced, in other words, by "symbols." "It was," Coleridge says, "only to overthrow the usurpation exercised in and through the senses, that the senses were miraculously appealed to" (p. 10). But if one remains enslaved to the miracle itself, one cannot come to know the truth it was meant to reveal. Once one has glimpsed the biblical truths, however, "the principles revealed . . . in the inspired writings render miracles superfluous" (p. 10).

This is, of course, consistent with what Coleridge wrote of miracles elsewhere. For Coleridge, it is of the essence of miracles not that they be contraventions of the laws of nature, such as the parting of the Red Sea or the raising of Lazarus, but that they mediate God's revelation to the beholder. A cloud in the sky or the birth of a child, perceived

---

[2] *LS*, p. 9. The full title of this work is *The Statesman's Manual; or, The Bible the Best Guide to Political Skill and Foresight; A Lay Sermon, Addressed to the Higher Classes of Society.* Hereafter in this chapter page references will be made parenthetically in the text.

in faith, can be as much a divine sign as the cleansing of a leper or the healing of a blind man. "Whether its cause be within or without the observed 'laws of nature,' the essential element of a miracle for Coleridge is that it be a divine sign, God's special means of speaking to man and drawing attention to His revelation."[3] As Coleridge wrote in one of his later notebooks, "What other definition does the term, Miracle, require or admit than 'Acts, Incidents, Appearances calculated to excite awe and wonder'? And what more fitted to impress the mind with awe and wonder, than Law? The Effects are *always* admirable; but when they are such as to direct the Beholder's mind to the *Agent* while his attention is drawn to the Work—to make him recognize the presence of the Law itself shining thro' the Effects—then do these most rightfully claim the name of Signs and Wonders!"[4]

Having turned our attention away from the miracles of the Bible, Coleridge asks us to focus on the nature of the biblical revelation itself. "The Hebrew legislator, and the other inspired poets, prophets, historians and moralists of the Jewish church," he says, "have two immense advantages in their favor" (p. 17). The first is that "their particular rules and prescripts flow directly and visibly from universal principles, as from a fountain; they flow from principles and ideas that are not so properly said to be confirmed by reason as to be reason itself!" Secondly, "from the very nature of these principles, as taught in the Bible, they are understood in exact proportion as they are believed and felt. The regulator is never separated from the main spring" (p. 17).

The first and most fundamental of these principles, Coleridge makes clear, is enunciated in the words of St. Paul: "WE ['that is, the human race,' Coleridge adds] LIVE BY FAITH."[5] Coleridge then goes on: "Whatever we do or know, that in kind is different from the brute creation, has its origin

---

[3] Barth, *Coleridge and Christian Doctrine*, p. 40.

[4] This quotation is taken, with permission, from one of Coleridge's still unpublished notebooks, Notebook 39, ff. 10–11 (c. 1826).

[5] See Rom.1:17 and Gal. 3:11.

in a determination of the reason to have faith and trust in itself. This, its first act of faith is scarcely less than identical with its own being. . . . It is . . . the realizing principle, the spiritual substratum of the whole complex body of truths. This primal act of faith is enunciated in the word, GOD: a faith not derived from experience, but its ground and source" (p. 18).

Perhaps one can best explain the link between these two seemingly disparate stages—the faith in one's self that is virtually "identical with one's own being" and its enunciation in the word *God*—by a phrase Coleridge uses in this context: "the imperative and oracular form of the inspired Scripture" (p. 18). The very form of the Scripture calls the reader to an acceptance both of the message and of the God who reveals it, as well as of the reader's empowerment by God—and therefore calls the reader (in the Pauline phrase) to "live by faith," seeing oneself and God in a single act of vision. As Coleridge goes on to insist, "Man alone was created in the image of God" (p. 19), because humankind alone is endowed with reason. In a marginal note on this passage, Coleridge wrote in a copy of *The Statesman's Manual* that Reason, as distinguished from mere "Understanding," is "that in the mind which from individual (or particular) <and contingent> facts and forms concludes universal, necessary, and permanent Truth."[6] Implicit here are that God is not separate from the truths revealed, and that in revealing truth God is at the same time revealing himself.

Coleridge's conception of "translucence" may be helpful here, and for this we must glance ahead a few pages in *The Statesman's Manual*, to the now familiar passage in which Coleridge distinguishes between allegory and symbol:

> Now an Allegory is but a translation of abstract notions into a picture-language which is itself nothing but an abstraction from objects of the senses. . . . On the other hand a Symbol . . . is characterized by a translucence of the Special in the Individual or of the General in the Especial or of the Univer-

---

[6] See *LS*, 19, n. 1.

sal in the General. Above all by the translucence of the Eternal through and in the Temporal. It always partakes of the Reality which it renders intelligible; and while it enunciates the whole, abides itself as a living part in that Unity, of which it is the representative. (p. 30)

The "Unity" of which Coleridge speaks is, of course, God, conceived of here (implicitly) as light: if a symbol of the Eternal is "translucent," then God is the light that passes through it—the Eternal revealing itself "through and in the Temporal."[7] Whether it be through a spokesman like Moses or Isaiah, an event like the dropping of the manna in the desert or David's slaying of Goliath, or the very act of Creation itself in all its wealth of detail, throughout the Bible the Eternal is constantly revealing itself through and in the Temporal. "In the Bible," Coleridge wrote, "every agent appears and acts as a self-subsisting individual: each has a life of its own, and yet all are one life" (p. 31). God is indeed distinct from Moses, from the manna, and even from the act of Creation, yet is not separate from them; God is united with them by his divine creative and abiding presence.[8] When light passes through a translucent medium—a stained-glass window, for instance—the light and the window, however distinguishable, are not separate. To use an-

---

[7] Tzvetan Todorov distinguishes helpfully between allegory as *transitive* and symbol as *intransitive*: "in allegory there is an instantaneous passage through the signifying face of the sign toward knowledge of what is signified, whereas in the symbol this face retains its proper value, its opacity. Allegory is transitive, symbols are intransitive—but in such a way that they do not cease to signify for all that; the symbol's intransitivity, in other words, goes hand in hand with its syntheticism. Thus the symbol speaks to perception (along with intellection); the allegory in effect speaks to intellection alone" (*Theories of Symbol*, p. 201). While Todorov's use of the term "opacity" may be misleading, I believe that implicit here is a view of allegory as transparent, symbol as translucent—since the symbol "retains its proper value" and yet does not "cease to signify."

[8] The conception is similar to Coleridge's view of the genius of Shakespeare, each of whose characters has a distinct and inimitable individuality, yet at the same time reveals the creative presence of Shakespeare: "In all his various characters, we still feel ourselves communing with the same human nature"; *FR*, I, 457.

other Coleridgean word we have seen before (in chapter 1): the two realities "interpenetrate." The multicolored beauty of the window is revealed in all the richness of its individuality, brought to life by the splendor of the light shining through it, while the light is (to borrow a phrase from Gerard Manley Hopkins) "sifted to suit our sight." In contemplating the stained-glass window, we are at the same time seeing the sunlight, not in a blinding glare too bright for our eyes, but softened—its unity broken into some of its component colors, so that our poor eyes can look upon it and live.

Some such conception is, clearly, implicit in Coleridge's notion of the "translucence" of the biblical symbols. The movement of the waters in Creation, the rainbow of the covenant with Noah, the pillar of fire and the sojourn in the desert, the chariot of Elijah and Job's whirlwind, the birth of the Baptist and the calming of the storm at sea, all not only reveal themselves and some truth *about* God but at the same time reveal God himself, working in and through these temporal realities. Thus, the agents and events of the Bible and the divine Author of them are, in Coleridgean terms, "translucent" to one another; the divine light shines through the stained-glass window of Scripture, so that we perceive both in a single act of vision. For, as Coleridge insists (in yet another telling metaphor), "the root is never detached from the ground" (p. 32).

If the "imperative and oracular form" of Scripture implies that God is not separate from the truths God reveals, it also implies that Scripture is at the same time empowering for the reader. The human reason's "primal act of faith" of which Coleridge speaks—which is "scarcely less than identical with its own being"—is, we recall, "enunciated in the word, God." If God is, as Coleridge insists, the Supreme Reason, the human being has a share in the same reason; it is precisely in this way, in fact, that humankind, alone within creation, was "created in the image of God" (p. 19). It is, one might say, reason calling out to reason, "imperatively and oracularly." As the human imagination shares in the eternal creative imagination of God—"a repetition in the finite mind of the eternal act of creation in the infinite I AM"[9]—so the finite human reason participates in the Supreme Reason, mediated through the "individual (or particular) and contingent facts and forms" that constitute the texture of sacred Scripture. After all, although it is true that the Bible is made up of a multitude of highly particularized people, moments, and events, it is also true that the "imperative and oracular form of the inspired Scripture is the form of reason itself in all things purely rational and moral" (p. 18).

Thus, the encounter between the Supreme Reason manifested in Scripture and the human reason of the reader is an encounter between God and God's image in humanity; as the human imagination receives its power from its participation in the divine eternal creative act, so does human reason receive power from the Supreme Reason. The human reason can "live by faith," that is, can "have faith and trust in itself" (p. 18), because it is in communion, through the "imperative and oracular form of the inspired Scripture," with the very being of God.

For Coleridge, this biblical principle—that "we live by faith"—and all the other principles that flow from it are inextricably bound up with *belief* and *feeling*; as he insists, "they are understood in exact proportion as they are believed and felt" (p. 17). The human understanding, Coleridge says, in its search for meaning, "snatches at truth, but is frustrated and disheartened by the fluctuating nature of its objects; its conclusions therefore are timid and uncertain, and it hath no way of giving permanence to things but by reducing them to abstractions" (p. 20). But the "imperative and oracular" force of the Bible calls us to knowledge by believing and feeling, and (as Coleridge says) "the principle of knowledge is likewise a spring and principle of action" (p. 20). Part of the difference is in the motive force: "The understanding," Coleridge goes on, "may suggest motives,

---

[9] *BL*, I, 304.

may avail itself of motives, and make judicious conjectures respecting the probable consequences of actions. But the knowledge taught in the Scriptures *produces* the motives, *involves* the consequences; and its highest formula is still: AS SURE AS GOD LIVETH, so will it be unto thee!" (p. 21).

Another key to Coleridge's "system" of scriptural knowledge may be found in the very unfashionable notion of enthusiasm.[10] "What is enthusiasm," he asks, "but the oblivion and swallowing-up of self in an object dearer than self, or in an idea more vivid?" (p. 23). There is, he admits, an "enthusiasm of wickedness," but "in the genuine enthusiasm of morals, religion, and patriotism, this enlargement and elevation of the soul above its mere self attest the presence, and accompany the intuition of ultimate PRINCIPLES alone. . . . Every idea is living, productive, [and] partaketh of infinity" (p. 23). In every perception of a truth—an idea—in Scripture, there is an implicit perception of God, since "every idea partaketh of infinity." The soul is linked with God by the very perception of truth in faith. In a single act of vision, the soul perceives both the truth and the source of that truth. In Coleridgean terms, nothing less than the imagination can encompass such knowledge, which in its *object* comprehends both the temporal and the eternal, and in its *function* involves intellect, will, and feelings. Only the imagination, not the Understanding, can express certain and living truth, truth that is its own validation. Only the symbols mediated by imagination can afford us the "enthusiasm" that allows us to go out of ourselves sufficiently to grasp a truth that is both ourselves and not ourselves, both ourselves and the ultimate source of ourselves.

In all of this, we must underscore again that Coleridge's conception of imagination (and the Coleridgean "Reason" that undergirds it) does depend upon an act of faith: an act of faith in ourselves as capable of knowing reality beyond

---

[10] It was Coleridge in 1816—not Emerson in his *Essays* of 1841, as is commonly assumed—who first said "nothing great was ever atcheived [*sic*] without enthusiasm"; see *LS*, p. 23.

ourselves, and of faith that there is a connaturality between our imagination and the infinite I AM; that our imagination is truly (as the *Biographia Literaria* has it) "a repetition in the finite mind of the eternal act of creation in the infinite I AM."

The problem Coleridge points to in his own day—to which his conceptions of Reason and imagination are a response—is that so many have lost faith not only in God but also in language; Reason and imagination have been replaced, all too often, by the mechanical Understanding: "The histories and political economy of the present and preceding century partake in the general contagion of its mechanic philosophy, and are the *product* of an unenlivened generalizing Understanding" (p. 28). Such histories in the Scripture, however, are "the living *educts* of the Imagination," which give birth to "a system of symbols, harmonious in themselves, and consubstantial with the truths, of which they are the *conductors*" (p. 29). It is significant that Coleridge italicizes three cognate words in this passage: *product*, *educts*, and *conductors*. The Understanding can give only a "product," something of its own making. The imagination, however, is seen as "giving birth" to symbols that are "educts," that is, are led forth from the truths of which they are the "conductors." The symbols are both "*e*ducts" and "*con*ductors": they are "led forth" from the truth and at the same time accompany that truth or, as it were, carry that truth with them. While the Understanding is a mechanical faculty, dealing (like the Fancy) with "fixities and definites," the imagination is an organic faculty, which can mediate actively between two modes of reality, even between the finite and the infinite. The "mechanic Understanding" can give only temporal fact or history; the imagination can offer the temporal in the light of the eternal. As Coleridge goes on to say of the Bible, "its contents present to us the stream of time continuous as Life and a symbol of Eternity" (p. 29).

Moreover, because the Bible is a work of imagination it shows us the relationship between parts and whole, the relationship of individuals to the whole sacred history. Coleridge says: "In the Scriptures therefore both Facts and Persons must of necessity have a two-fold significance, a past and a future, a temporal and a perpetual, a particular and a universal application. They must be at once Portraits and Ideals." Unlike the "dead letter" of the present age, the biblical symbols, as works of imagination, are "characterized by . . . the translucence of the Eternal through and in the Temporal" (p. 30). We have seen the importance of that very Coleridgean word *translucence*: the same light shines through both, the temporal and the eternal, without either one blocking out the other; the human and the divine are apprehended in a single act.

But if this is so, then there is, Coleridge claims, a similar relationship among the *individuals* in the Bible; if they are all images of God—all "translucent" to the light of God—then there is a deep underlying unity among them: "In the Bible every agent appears and acts as a self-subsisting individual: each has a life of its own, and yet all are one life" (p. 31). All are one because all are rooted in God: "the root is never detached from the ground" (p. 32).

The organic analogy is everywhere implicit in *The Statesman's Manual*. I deliberately say "analogy" (which I use in the philosophical sense), not "metaphor," for Coleridge insists on the reality of the organic relationship between humankind and God, between the human imagination and the eternal creative act. The Bible "differs from all the books of Greek philosophy," he insists, because it "doth not affirm a Divine Nature only, but a God: and not a God only, but the living God" (pp. 32–33). Implicit here is what most crucially characterizes Coleridge's view of the scriptural imagination: his belief that the Bible, perhaps uniquely, everywhere affirms the *source* of the imaginative power even as it exercises it.

Coleridge's claims for the Bible are indeed awesome. In his view, the Bible can, by placing us in touch with the sources of imaginative power, bring God to birth, as it were, within us, for the Idea mediated by the imagination is "that most glorious birth of the God-like within us" (p. 50). There is, he says, "hidden mystery in every, the minutest, form of existence." Such a mystery "contemplated under the relations of time" appears as "an infinite ascent of Causes, and prospectively as an interminable progression of Effects"; contemplated in space, it is seen as "a law of action and re-action." However, he goes on, "this same mystery freed from the phenomena of Time and Space, and seen in the depth of *real* Being, reveals itself to the pure Reason as the actual immanence of ALL IN EACH" (pp. 49–50).

Perhaps what Coleridge envisioned as the imaginative power of the scriptures to put us in touch with the divine reality may be glimpsed in this passage from the end of *The Statesman's Manual*:

> O what a mine of undiscovered treasures, what a new world of Power and Truth would the Bible promise to our future meditation, if in some gracious moment one solitary text of all its inspired contents should but dawn upon us in the pure untroubled brightness of an IDEA, that most glorious birth of the God-like within us, which even as the Light, its material symbol, reflects itself from a thousand surfaces, and flies homeward to its Parent Mind enriched with a thousand forms, itself above form and still remaining in its own simplicity and identity! (p. 50)

Here indeed is life begetting life—the "birth of the God-like within us"—the creative human imagination drawing life from its source, the infinite and everlasting creative act of God.

7

Symbol and Romanticism

ONE OF THE MOST SPIRITED DISCUSSIONS of symbolism in the nineteenth century is Charles Feidelson's *Symbolism and American Literature*. Feidelson's discussion of Emerson, Melville, Hawthorne, Poe, and Whitman begins, perhaps inevitably, with "the problem of romanticism." These writers were not Romantic, Feidelson says, but they did inherit "the basic problem of romanticism: the vindication of imaginative thought in a world grown abstract and material."[1] We are back to one of Coleridge's deepest concerns, as we saw in chapter 2, that "it is among the miseries of the present age that it recognizes no medium between *Literal* and *Metaphorical*."[2] The world had indeed grown "abstract and material," and the answer did lie in "imaginative thought," which required "justification" in the eyes of such a world. Such a world can tolerate, even use, allegory, which Coleridge called "but a translation of abstract notions into a picture-language which is itself nothing but an abstraction from objects of the senses."[3] But it cannot tolerate the inconclusiveness, the mystery, the "translucence" of symbol. Words should have hard edges, like the world.

In Feidelson's view, Hawthorne was caught between two worlds—the acceptable world of matter-of-fact reality and a world of mysteries that are somehow beyond the telling, "the common-sense objective world" and "the private vision." He was caught between a world of allegory and a world of symbol. For, Feidelson says, "it is in the nature of allegory, as opposed to symbolism, to beg the question of absolute reality. The allegorist avails himself of a formal

---

[1] *Symbolism and American Literature* (Chicago, 1953), p. 4.
[2] *LS*, p. 30.
[3] *LS*, p. 30.

correspondence between 'ideas' and 'things,' both of which he assumes as given; he need not inquire whether either sphere is 'real' or whether, in the final analysis, reality consists in their interaction."[4]

How Hawthorne triumphantly overcame, in the best of his work, this "debilitating conflict—between the symbolist and the allegorist" (p. 14)—is not part of our story. What is important for our purpose is that he is a case in point—in the work of a great artist—of the deep opposition between the allegorical and the symbolic modes of thought. And as it was with Hawthorne, so it was with Coleridge. It was impossible for Coleridge, with his passion for unity of apprehension of the world, to accept a merely "formal correspondence" between "ideas" and "things." Not only must he affirm the reality of both because both are part of his experience, but reality most emphatically does consist in their interaction. Coleridge could never "beg the question of absolute reality."

There comes a point, however, at which we must part company with Feidelson in our discussion. For Feidelson, the "symbolistic method" of which he speaks is essentially a post-Romantic phenomenon—"closer to modern notions of symbolic reality than to romantic egoism" (p. 4). But, surely, this stereotype of Romantic "egoism" reflects little of the complexity of vision we have seen in Coleridge and Wordsworth. Their visions flow from a much more complex source—in fact, from a source no less exalted than the imagination, the symbol-making faculty, which "brings the whole soul of man into activity." Whatever may be said of Hawthorne, in Coleridge and Wordsworth it is precisely the symbolic mode of apprehension that constitutes them as Romantic. Everything else that is part of their Romanticism—its egoism, its emphasis on feeling, its freedom—is subsumed under the symbolic mode.

What Feidelson does do for us, however, is to underscore the importance of the distinction Coleridge insists upon be-

[4] Feidelson, p. 8.

tween allegory and symbol. We have talked much of symbol; it is time now to speak about allegory.

There is, admittedly, cause for a certain measure of embarrassment about Coleridge's views on allegory. The difficulty is not with his conception of its meaning; his notion of it, given its clearest formulation in one of his lectures of 1818, is unexceptionable:

> We may then safely define allegoric writing as the employment of one set of agents and images with actions and accompaniments correspondent, so as to convey, while in disguise, either moral qualities or conceptions of the mind that are not in themselves objects of the senses, or other images, agents, actions, fortunes, and circumstances, so that the difference is everywhere presented to the eye or imagination while the likeness is suggested to the mind; and this connectedly so that the parts combine to form a consistent whole.[5]

The difficulty comes with Coleridge's judgment of individual allegories. Having decided that allegory is a weaker form of poetry, he is left with the problem of what to say of the great writers who are commonly thought of as allegorists, poets like Dante, Spenser, and Bunyan. His solution is simplicity itself: these writers are great in spite of the fact that they are sometimes allegorists, and they are allegorists far less often than we assume. Where their art is most successful, we can happily forget that it may be allegory. "If the allegoric personage be strongly individualized so as to interest us, we cease to think of it as allegory—and if it does not interest us, it had better be away." Of "that admirable Allegory, the first Part of *Pilgrim's Progress*, which de-

---

[5] Lecture III of 1818, in *Coleridge's Miscellaneous Criticism*, ed. Thomas Middleton Raysor (Cambridge, Mass., 1936), p. 30. The definition quoted above does not appear in the text of the lecture established by Foakes (*LL*, II, 85–105). Kathleen Coburn's assessment of the lecture's complicated textual history is helpful: "[Henry Nelson Coleridge] may have been approximately right about the content of that lecture; he appears to have produced a reasonable pastiche from a mixture of scraps of actual reports, loose sheets of mss, verbal accounts, notebook entries, and marginalia"; *The Notebooks of Samuel Taylor Coleridge*, ed. Kathleen Coburn, 4 vols. to date III, 4501 (Princeton, 1955–), note.

lights every one," he can insist that "the interest is so great
that spite of all the writer's attempts to force the allegoric
purpose on the Reader's mind by his strange names—Old
Stupidity of the Tower of Honesty, &c &c—his piety was
baffled by his Genius, and the Bunyan of Parnassus had the
better of Bunyan of the Conventicle." As for Spenser, "the
dullest and most defective parts of Spenser are those in
which we are compelled to think of his agents as allegories."[6]

Coleridge's approach to Dante as allegorist is rather different: it is simply to deny that he is really an allegorist at
all. "The Divina Commedia is a system of moral, political,
and theological truths, with arbitrary personal exemplifications, which are not, in my opinion, allegorical."[7] In order
to understand his view of Dante we must go back a bit in
the same lecture. For the Greeks, Coleridge says, the end
was the finite form. With Christianity the reverse is true:
"Finites, even the human form, must, in order to satisfy the
mind, be brought into connexion with, and be in fact symbolical of, the infinite."[8] From this resulted "two great Effects—a combination of Poetry with *Doctrines*—and (by
turning the mind inward on its own *essence* instead of its
circumstances and communities) with sentiment."[9] It is these
"two great effects" which bring it about that Dante is not
essentially an allegorist. What he is, in Coleridge's view,
will perhaps come clear from a culling of phrases from
Coleridge's discussion of the characteristics of Dante's

---

[6] *LL*, II, 102–103.

[7] Lecture X of 1818, in *Miscellaneous Criticism*, p. 150. The text of
this passage in Foakes (*LL*, II, 400) provides a less emphatic dismissal
of allegory: ". . . personal exemplifications—<the punishments indeed
allegorical perhaps>"; but see also Foakes's earlier note 7 on this lecture:
"Coleridge's disagreements [with Schlegel] may have been, as Kathleen
Coburn suggests in [*Collected Notebooks*] III 4498n, firstly that Schlegel
placed a high valuation on allegory, and C a low one (cf. Lect. 7, below,
n 9) and secondly that C rejected the notion that Dante's poem was essentially an allegory . . ." (*LL*, II, 398).

[8] *Miscellaneous Criticism*, p. 148. Foakes omits "and be in fact symbolical of" (*LL*, II, 399).

[9] *LL*, II, 399.

poetry. "The Images in Dante are not only taken from obvious nature, and are intelligible to all, but are ever conjoined with the universal feeling received from them, and therefore affect the general feelings of all men."[10] And again: "Dante does not so much elevate your thoughts as send them down deeper."[11] Still again: "He thus takes the thousand delusive forms of a nature worse than chaos, having no reality but from the passions which they excite, and compels them into the service of the permanent."[12] Clearly, Dante is, for Coleridge, a poet not of allegory but of symbol, trafficking not with "fixities and definites" but with mystery.

It would be foolish to deny Coleridge's shortsightedness on the matter of allegory. It is clear that his distaste for allegory arises from a preoccupation with the baleful effects of bad allegory: the work of mere fancy and of the mechanical understanding. Unfortunately, this distaste led him to a summary dismissal of all allegory; had he been able to distinguish between good and bad, his criticism might have been all the richer for it. As it is, his attempts to explain away the allegorical elements of poets he obviously loved seem more than a bit absurd.

This failure on Coleridge's part, however, should not be allowed to stand in the way of an appreciation of his distinction between allegory and symbol. Yet there are those who have done so. In *Dark Conceit: The Making of Allegory*, Edwin Honig writes of Coleridge: "As a principal source of the modern opposition to the concept of allegory, he is probably responsible—because his strictures on the subject have been taken too literally or misapplied—for instigating numerous pedantic distinctions between symbolism and allegory."[13] On the contrary, it is because his views on sym-

---

[10] *Miscellaneous Criticism*, p. 152. Foakes omits the phrase "and therefore affect the general feelings of all men" (*LL*, II, 401).

[11] *Miscellaneous Criticism*, p. 152. This beautiful phrase is absent from Foakes's text.

[12] *Miscellaneous Criticism*, p. 155. The version of this passage in Foakes (*LL*, II, 402) is considerably less fluid.

[13] *Dark Conceit: The Making of Allegory* (New York, 1966), p. 44.

bol have not been taken literally enough that Coleridge has so often been misunderstood.

There is an anti-Romanticism in Honig's view—distant kin to the milder form in Feidelson—that is more than a little disturbing:

> For the social hierarchy under God, the Romantics substituted an esthetic hierarchy based on the prerogatives of the man of feeling, the immoralist, the artist, the confidence trickster. The Romantics could easily dismiss the Lord of Creation for a God of Love, Sympathetic Nature, or the Demon of the Absolute. Instead of Bunyan's plodding Christian earning his heavenly reward by imitating the life of Christ, they invoked a monstrous egoist who lavishly loved woman, knowledge, power, or freedom more than the world, and who, when frustrated, sought to impoverish it by his suicide.

Thus, he concludes: "Setting aside prescribed systems of axiomatic interpretation, they expounded the psychological or mythological brief which interpreted artistic creation as an original and self-inclusive act" (pp. 40–41).

Whatever may be said of this as a summary view of "the Romantics"—it obviously reveals the simplifications of any epitome of such a complex movement as Romanticism—what is particularly disturbing about it is that in the context of Honig's book it is Coleridge who is seen as the key to it all. It is Coleridge precisely, and very emphatically, as the mediator of Kant and Kantian attitudes and values. For the Romantic, Honig believes, what is crucial in Kant is "the stress upon the subjectivity of all experience." For, he goes on, "unlike Plato and Aristotle, Kant does not say that the important thing is nature as the symbol of God's capacity, but the capacity in the individual man to discern the beautiful and to introduce the sublime into the idea of nature" (p. 43).

It would be ridiculous to deny the obvious Kantian strains in English Romanticism, but to invoke the name of Kant is not to explain the complex phenomenon of Romanticism.

This *caveat* is especially urgent in the case of Coleridge. Surely, we may acknowledge Coleridge's debt to Kant, as he himself does very clearly in the *Biographia Literaria*, without turning him into a Kantian. The opposition set up by Honig between Plato and Kant, true though it is in itself, is particularly inappropriate in the context of Coleridge, and indeed of English Romanticism generally. For all the influence of Kant's subjectivism, Coleridge—and for that matter most of the English Romantics—remain far more Platonist than Kantian. It should be abundantly clear by now that the act of imagination—symbol-making—was for Coleridge not merely (in Honig's words) "an original and self-inclusive act," but also an act of surpassing openness to reality other than the self. Like too many other commentators, Honig fails to take account of a crucial difference between Kant and Coleridge on the nature and reality of ideas and, therefore, of symbols.

To explain this difference, we must briefly retrace some ground partly covered earlier. For Coleridge a symbol is an idea; although by its nature an idea is supersensuous, in symbol it is bodied forth in sense images. A symbol results from the conjoined working of reason and understanding. Reason (the human faculty of the supersensuous) and understanding (the faculty that knows according to the senses) work together under the direction of the imagination to produce symbol. As Coleridge wrote in the *Biographia Literaria*, "an IDEA, in the *highest* sense of that word, cannot be conveyed but by a *symbol*." [14] We have seen more than once the classic definition of symbol in *The Statesman's Manual*. Referring to the human aspects of the Bible—"the history of Men," the "influence of individual Minds," "national morals and manners"—Coleridge says they are "the living *educts* of the Imagination; of that reconciling and mediatory power, which incorporating the Reason in Images of the Sense, and organizing (as it were) the flux of the Senses by the permanence and self-circling energies of the Reason,

---

[14] *BL*, I, 156.

gives birth to a system of symbols, harmonious in themselves, and consubstantial with the truths, of which they are
the *conductors*. . . . Its contents present to us the stream of
time continuous as Life and a symbol of Eternity."[15] The
supersensuous truths that reason knows can be bodied forth
in "Images of the Sense" only because the two are consubstantial. The world of transcendent reality—the world of
ideas—shares a community of being with the world of temporal, sensible things. Eternal and temporal, ideal and sensible, are consubstantial one with the other. Thus, the two can
be known, by symbol, in a single act of perception, because
a symbol is (in the now familiar quotation) "characterized
by a translucence of the Special in the Individual or of the
General in the Especial or of the Universal in the General.
Above all by the translucence of the Eternal through and in
the Temporal. It always partakes of the Reality which it renders intelligible; and while it enunciates the whole, abides
itself as a living part in that Unity, of which it is the representative."[16]

All this is a far cry from the subjectivism of Kant. For
Kant, all our ideas beyond mere sense experience (whether
the transcendental ideas of pure reason or the ideas of practical reason) remain merely regulative—a means of ordering
our experience of the world. Neither through the a priori
categories of sense experience (space and time) nor through
ideas can the human mind be said to "know" reality beyond
the self. For Coleridge, on the other hand, ideas, and therefore symbols, are not merely regulative but also constitutive. Consubstantial as they are with "the truths of which
they are the *conductors*," symbols convey true apprehension not only of the self but also of reality beyond the self,
both supersensuous reality (because it involves the work of
reason) and sensible reality (because it also subsumes the
work of understanding). At least in a Coleridgean perspective, Romanticism is no mere subjectivism. It is not simply

[15] *LS*, p. 29.
[16] *LS*, p. 30.

a way of feeling but also a way of knowing—and of knowing not just oneself but whatever is. Allegory may (to return
to Charles Feidelson's phrase) "beg the question of absolute
reality"—assuming a merely formal correspondence between ideas and things—but true symbol, in Coleridge's
sense, can never do so.

C. S. Lewis, in *The Allegory of Love*, takes us a bit further
when he says that "symbolism is a mode of thought, but
allegory is a mode of expression."[17] To discover what he
means will require us again to take a few steps backward:

> It is of the very nature of thought and language to represent
> what is immaterial in picturable terms. . . . This fundamental
> equivalence between the immaterial and the material may be
> used by the mind in two ways. . . . On the one hand you can
> start with an immaterial fact, such as the passions which you
> actually experience, and can then invent *visibilia* to express
> them. If you are hesitating between an angry retort and a soft
> answer, you can express your state of mind by inventing a
> person called *Ira* with a torch and letting her contend with
> another invented person called *Patientia*. This is allegory. . . .
> But there is another way of using the equivalence, which is
> almost the opposite of allegory, and which I would call sacra-
> mentalism or symbolism. If our passions, being immaterial,
> can be copied by material inventions, then it is possible that
> our material world in its turn is the copy of an invisible
> world. . . . The attempt to read that something else through
> sensible imitations, to see the archetype in the copy, is what
> I mean by symbolism or sacramentalism. (pp. 44–45)

Symbol is "a mode of thought," of thinking one's way
more deeply into what is real. In applying this to Romanticism, we should perhaps hasten to add that the "archetype"
the symbolic poet is trying to see is not merely a Platonic
archetype in the noumenal world, the world of the "Divine
Ideas." To be sure, the Romantic poet—Coleridge least of
all—does not exclude the possibility of such vision. But

---

[17] *The Allegory of Love: A Study in Medieval Tradition* (New York,
1958), p. 48.

"archetype," for the Romantics, must be taken to include the inner archetypes as well, the archetypes of the self as well as the archetypes of eternity. Nothing is excluded from the symbolic poet's search. What is important is that the poet is always searching for deeper and broader reality, and symbol is the mode of that searching. As Lewis says, "The difference between the two can hardly be exaggerated. The allegorist leaves the given—his own passions—to talk of that which is confessedly less real, which is a fiction. The symbolist leaves the given to find that which is more real" (p. 45). Nor are we distorting Lewis's thought by translating it from its medieval context, for he goes on: "But of course the poetry of symbolism does not find its greatest expression in the Middle Ages at all, but rather in the time of the romantics" (p. 46).

C. S. Lewis has brought us full circle, too, to the sacramental nature of symbol. Edwin Honig's problem—in finding Coleridge's distinction between allegory and symbol merely "pedantic"—comes from his failure to understand the essentially sacramental nature of symbol in Coleridge's thought. It is far from a matter of taking Coleridge too literally; on the contrary, the problem comes from not taking him literally enough. Coleridge means what he says: the symbol truly partakes of the reality it represents.

One may ask if even such a distinguished critic as M. H. Abrams takes full account of this sacramental aspect of Romantic symbol. In the context of Abrams's *Natural Supernaturalism*, no truly sacramental view of reality is possible for the Romantics. Too deep a rift has grown between the old Christian truths and the new secular metaphysics; the "characteristic concepts and patterns of Romantic philosophy and literature are a displaced and reconstituted theology, or else a secularized form of devotional experience."[18] There is no room for symbol, in Coleridge's sense, in such a world. There can be allegory—a fictionalized correspon-

---

[18] *Natural Supernaturalism: Tradition and Revolution in Romantic Literature* (New York, 1971), p. 65.

dence to worlds that may or may not be real—but there can be no symbol, because there is no true community of being.

Our primary concern is with Coleridge, and Abrams's application of his view to Coleridge is consistent: "Coleridge, who from the time of his maturity was a professing Christian, carried on a lifetime's struggle to save what seemed to him the irreducible minimum of the Christian creed within an essentially secular metaphysical system" (p. 67). Lurking beneath this judgment is an unwillingness to admit that Coleridge's "system" was what he made it, not Schellingian, not Kantian, but Coleridgean. We are faced, yet again, with the legacy of René Wellek, who was never able to grant Coleridge the freedom to do with his great German predecessors what they did with theirs—shape something new out of them. In such a view, German thought must always lie like an undigested lump in Coleridge's stomach.

Obviously, our contention throughout this book has been quite other: that, whatever its shortcomings in conception and formulation, Coleridge was able to evolve, if not fully to shape, a generally consistent body of thought that is at once religious and secular. Indeed, this is precisely the role played by symbol in his thought: to reconcile opposites, or what seem to be opposites, including the secular and the religious, the temporal and the eternal. All reality is consubstantial with all other reality—that is the central mystery.

Nor is it only Coleridge who suffers from this view of an unbridgeable chasm between the natural and the supernatural. Carlyle, from whom the phrase "natural supernaturalism" is taken, is himself portrayed as essentially a humanist. Yet I cannot think that Abrams's reading is faithful to Sartor Resartus. In Professor Teufelsdröckh's chapter entitled "Natural Supernaturalism," Carlyle is talking about miracles, as the traditional incursion of the divine realm into the human, the supernatural into the natural. In its preoccupation with supernatural miracles, humanity has blinded itself to the even greater daily miracles around us in the world of nature: "The true inexplicable God-revealing Miracle lies in this, that I can stretch forth my hand at all; that I have free Force to clutch aught therewith."[19] The point is not that natural and supernatural are divorced from each other, that divine and human are no longer at one, that the Godhead does not reveal itself. Quite the contrary. The point is that God is revealed even more intimately, more humanly, than we have allowed ourselves to think. "Then sawest thou that this fair universe, were it in the meanest province thereof, is in very deed the star-domed City of God; that through every star, through every grass-blade, and most through every Living Soul, the glory of a present God still beams. But Nature, which is the Time-vesture of God, and reveals Him to the wise, hides Him from the foolish."[20] Clearly, God is not absent from this world; God is, as Carlyle says, "a present God."

Even symbol itself falls under Professor Teufelsdröckh's scrutiny, and his pages on symbol are wonderfully Coleridgean both in content and in spirit: "In the Symbol proper, what we can call a Symbol, there is ever, more or less distinctly and directly, some embodiment and revelation of the Infinite; the Infinite is made to blend itself with the Finite, to stand visible, and as it were, attainable there. . . . The Universe is but one vast Symbol of God; nay if thou wilt have it, what is man himself but a Symbol of God?"[21]

Abrams contends—quoting Carlyle's phrase, but referring it to the Romantic movement—"the general tendency was, in diverse degrees and ways, to naturalize the supernatural and to humanize the divine."[22] But is not Carlyle's point—and Coleridge's—just the opposite: that the natural is supernaturalized, the human is divinized? Both Carlyle and Coleridge must have seen that there is really nothing new in this. It is not a radical break with the past but an imaginative return to an earlier orthodoxy. For Coleridge, it had happened with

[19] Thomas Carlyle, *Sartor Resartus: The Life and Opinions of Herr Teufelsdröckh*, ed. Charles Frederick Harrold (Garden City, N.Y., 1937), Book III, chap. 8, p. 262.
[20] Carlyle, Book III, chap. 8, p. 264.
[21] Carlyle, Book III, chap. 3, p. 220.
[22] *Natural Supernaturalism*, p. 68.

the Incarnation of Christ; the world became a sacrament, a symbol. For Carlyle, although his commitment to doctrinal Christianity was long behind him, the world was still sacramental, and Christ was, at the least, its highest poet: "Our highest Orpheus walked in Judea, eighteen-hundred years ago: his sphere-melody, flowing in wild native tones, took captive the ravished souls of men; and, being of a true sphere-melody, still flows and sounds, though now with thousandfold accompaniments, and rich symphonies, through all our hearts; and modulates, and divinely leads them."[23]

Is it possible that the divine is not quite as lost in the Romantic period as one might think? Is it possible that it has been "relocated," so to speak, that it has been rediscovered where it has always been, in the world of nature and in the heart of humankind? The transcendent God of the eighteenth century has been found to be immanent in creation as well. If so, then it might be said that what has been lost is not the sacramental sense, but the too simple clarities of the allegorical sense. If we keep our meaning of "sacramental" broad enough to mean not only symbolic of supernatural reality but also symbolic of the inner reality of the self—sacrament in the broadest kind of way—then we may contend that the sacramental sense is very much alive not only in Coleridge and Carlyle but in the whole range of Romantic writers.

Yet it may be, then, that there is a sense in which Abrams's phrase is true—that the divine has been humanized. Gone are the simple clarities of allegory, leaving religion more mysterious, more faithful to the limitations of human perception. For Coleridge, Wordsworth, and Blake there is greater mystery in some form of Christianity; for others, like Shelley and Keats, there is greater mystery in

---

[23] Carlyle, Book III, chap. 8, p. 263. A comment of G. B. Tennyson is perhaps to the point here. He finds that, although Carlyle was "doctrinally no Christian," yet, because he "conceived of a higher force outside space and time, his orientation remained basically Christian." *"Sartor" Called "Resartus"* (Princeton, 1965), p. 318.

the sacrament of human experience itself. In any case, there is symbol. In any case, there is a greater faithfulness to the mysteries of human experience, as well as—for the Christians among them—to the vision of incarnate divinity.

Of course, such a view of symbol need not, indeed should not, be tied too tightly to the specifically Christian doctrine of the Incarnation. It means different things to different poets, as James Boulger has insisted.[24] Coleridge's view of symbol flows from a deeply Christian view of creation. For him, symbol proceeds, after all, from the imagination, which is "a repetition in the finite mind of the eternal act of creation in the infinite I ᴀᴍ."[25] But in all "the highest Romantic poetry," Boulger observes, there is always at least "the struggle to idealize and unify," which "leads to poetry of the original moment, the special insight of the soul, expressed in nature symbols which mediate by partaking of the numinous or sacred as well as the physical through the power of the artist's imagination."[26] These include, for example, "Wordsworth's many natural symbols which become numinous and imply the 'I ᴀᴍ' beyond the power of language. The tenors are vague terms for the 'I ᴀᴍ'— presence, something, immortal Spirit, Solitude, Sentiment of Being, and so on. The vehicles are the mountains, lonely figures, ruined monasteries, crosses, idiots, and the like" (p. 21). There is a broad range of reference for symbols in the Romantics, Boulger argues: "The 'I ᴀᴍ' of the later Coleridge is specifically Christian, Wordsworth's vaguely so. I venture to guess that Blake's ultimate Ideas and mediating images are close to those of Coleridge" (pp. 21–22). For others, there is no specifically Christian reference, but "the search for the numinous is identical in all the great Romantics, and always carried on by means of symbolism" (p. 21).

This "search for the numinous" may take many forms: an affirmation of faith, the gropings and glimpses of the

---

[24] "Coleridge on Imagination Revisited," *The Wordsworth Circle*, 4 (1973), 13–24.

[25] *BL*, I, 304.

[26] Boulger, p. 21.

sacred within oneself, the aspirations for an ideal world beyond the self, visionary glimpses of the sacred in another
person or in the sublimity of nature. But whatever form it
takes, it is a search that is finally beyond the power of words
or of mere metaphor. Even symbol can never fully capture
it, but it can begin to express and embrace it.

If this symbolism is not always specifically the sacrament
that reveals the Creator-God—Coleridge's "repetition in the
finite mind of the eternal act of creation in the infinite I
AM"—it is always at least the sacrament of the human experience, including experience of the numinous. If it is not
always the sacramental encounter with the mystery of the
infinite, it is at least a sacramental encounter with the mystery of one's deepest self, where, Coleridge might add, God
also dwells.

What we have seen of the poetry of Wordsworth and
Coleridge is a reflection and confirmation of all this. Their
poetry, at its most intense, is essentially a "search for the
numinous." As we said earlier, symbol-making for Coleridge—and symbol-perceiving—is essentially a religious
act. This does not always involve what a theologian would
call an act of theological faith. It may be, to be sure, whether
explicitly or implicitly, an expression of faith in a transcendent deity; but it may be only a glimpse of the sacred within
one's deepest self, or the aspiration for an ideal world beyond the self, or a moment of vision of the numinous in the
sublimity of nature. In any case, it invariably culminates
in symbolic vision, for only by symbol can the indefinable
"numinous" be articulated at all. "An IDEA, in the *highest*
sense of that word, cannot be conveyed but by a *symbol. . . .*"

We should add at once that the search for the numinous
that is expressed in symbol is at the same time more than a
search. It is an encounter; it is a search that is already in
some measure successful. The "search" is a struggle to articulate what has already been grasped without words—
what has been felt in the bones, what has been dreamt, what
has been glimpsed in vision. The search is for words, words
to express this numinous "other." The search is to articulate

an encounter, an encounter with the sacred, which has already taken place and yet takes place still in and around the symbol.

We have spoken much of "encounter," and yet the terms of this encounter have perhaps not always been clear. It may be that this is necessarily the case, since the encounter takes place at more than one level. There is the encounter between the poet and the reader, for which the poem is setting and catalyst; the poem is both the common ground and the energizing force of the meeting. We said earlier that symbolic language is "fiduciary," that it evokes an act of faith and trust on the part of the reader. As L. C. Knights has said, symbol "takes its meaning from a context: but—as it were—overlapping with the given context is the context of each individual's developing life experience, and the full meaning—the generative power—only exists in so far as this too is in some way—powerfully or subtly—affected."[27] The symbolic experience, on one level, is an encounter between the experience of the poet and the experience of the reader. To this extent it is definable: this poet, this reader.

But there is another encounter. The poet's experience itself is often an encounter between himself or herself and the sacred—the numinous "other"—whether discovered within or outside one's self. It is in and through our encounter with the poet's experience that we, too, encounter the numinous. This more primal encounter is, as we have suggested, even less susceptible of definition than the encounter of poet and reader. It is the very stuff of which the symbolic poem is made.

Since we gave considerable attention to Coleridge's views on the symbolic nature of scriptural truth, and since for Coleridge biblical symbol was the prototype of all symbolic representation, it will come as no surprise if we call this encounter with the numinous a deeply "biblical" kind

---

[27] "Idea and Symbol: Some Hints from Coleridge," in *Coleridge: A Collection of Critical Essays*, ed. Kathleen Coburn (Englewood Cliffs, N.J., 1967), p. 116.

of encounter. M. H. Abrams has very well noted that "we pay inadequate heed to the extent and persistence with which the writings of Wordsworth and his English contemporaries reflect not only the language and rhythms but also the design, the imagery, and many of the central moral values of the Bible."[28] He then goes on to make up for some of this inadequacy by discussing many of these biblical elements of Romantic poetry. But beyond common moral values, beyond design and imagery, even beyond language and rhythm, there is a still deeper biblical dimension in Romantic poetry. It is what Erich Auerbach calls "background."

Auerbach begins his book *Mimesis: The Representation of Reality in Western Literature* by contrasting two scenes. The first is the lovely scene in Book 19 of the *Odyssey* when Odysseus has come home at last and the old housekeeper Euryclea, who had been his nurse as a boy, recognizes him by a scar on this thigh. The whole scene, Auerbach comments,

> is scrupulously externalized and narrated in leisurely fashion. The two women [Penelope and the old woman] express their feelings in copious direct discourse. Feelings though they are, with only a slight admixture of the most general considerations upon human destiny, the syntactical connection between part and part is perfectly clear, no contour is blurred. There is also room and time for orderly, perfectly well-articulated, uniformly illuminated descriptions of implements, ministrations, and gestures; even in the dramatic moment of recognition, Homer does not omit to tell the reader that it is with his right hand that Odysseus takes the old woman by the throat to keep her from speaking, at the same time that he draws her closer to him with his left. Clearly outlined, brightly and uniformly illuminated, men and things stand out in a realm where everything is visible; and not less clear— wholly expressed, orderly even in their ardor—are the feelings and thoughts of the persons involved.[29]

The main point is that everything is in the foreground. As Auerbach says, "What he narrates is for the time being the

---

[28] *Natural Supernaturalism*, p. 32.
[29] *Mimesis: The Representation of Reality in Western Literature* (Princeton, 1953), pp. 1–2.

only present, and fills both the stage and the reader's mind completely" (p. 3). There is no background; everything is in the foreground.

Auerbach contrasts with this the story of Abraham's sacrifice of Isaac (Genesis 22). Unexpectedly and mysteriously, God enters the scene, in an unspecified place, and calls out to Abraham. We are given no reason for this sudden call to undergo a terrible trial, nor does it seem important that any be given. What is important is Abraham's response to the moral dilemma in which he is placed. A journey is made, but no description is given—only the details needed to complete the story. As Auerbach says: "In this atmosphere it is unthinkable that an implement, a landscape through which the travelers passed, the serving-men, or the ass, should be described, that their origin or descent or material or appearance or usefulness should be set forth in terms of praise; they do not even admit an adjective: they are serving-men, ass, wood, and knife, and nothing else, without an epithet; they are there to serve the end which God has commanded; what in other respects they were, are, or will be, remains in darkness" (p. 7). The whole story "remains mysterious and 'fraught with background' " (p. 9).

Because so much is merely suggested, there is a sense in the biblical story of another reality, a "background" that is somehow linked with the spare narrative of the foreground. The Homeric poems are more immediate. There is a great joy in physical action, and the poet clearly delights in making it present to us. There are battles and hunts, banquets, athletic contests, housekeeping chores—all sorts of absorbing physical details that are loved for themselves. By portraying them so powerfully, the poet makes us love them, too. Auerbach goes on: "The oft-repeated reproach that Homer is a liar takes nothing from his effectiveness, he does not need to base his story on historical reality, his reality is powerful enough in itself; it ensnares us, weaving its web around us, and that suffices him. And this 'real' world into which we are lured, exists for itself, contains nothing but itself; the Homeric poems conceal nothing. . . . Homer can

be analyzed . . . but he cannot be interpreted" (p. 11). The
biblical story, precisely because it suggests more than it
says, draws us into itself in a different way. Because a background is constantly and mysteriously present before us, we
are drawn to move beyond the reality of the foreground to
investigate and question the reality of the mysterious background.

What we have here are, clearly, two quite different ways
of representing reality in art. Whatever differences there
may be between the biblical and the Romantic modes—one
difference will surely be that there is considerably more attention to detail in Romantic poetry—Romantic poetry remains essentially biblical in its representation of reality; at
least as much is suggested as is expressed. As Heinz Politzer remarks of the symbolic work of Kafka, "clefts, cracks,
and crevices open, revealing the depth behind the realistic
detail."[30] Romantic poetry exists in a world of two realities:
the reality of foreground and the mysterious, finally impenetrable, reality of background. This reality of background is
what we have called "the numinous." We might say of the
Romantic "numinous" what Auerbach says of the biblical
story of Abraham and Isaac: "Far from seeking, like
Homer, merely to make us forget our own reality for a few
hours, it seeks to overcome our own reality: we are to fit our
own life into its world, feel ourselves to be elements in its
structure of universal history."[31] The Romantic encounter
with the numinous—whether in transcendent deity or in the
sublimity of nature or in the primal self—is, like the biblical
awareness of transcendent background, as much challenge
and confrontation as encounter. Like the Ancient Mariner,
we are led by symbolic encounter into sometimes fearful
worlds within and outside ourselves that challenge what we
are and confront us with what we might become.

We should not be surprised, I suppose, that Romanticism

---

[30] *Franz Kafka: Parable and Paradox*, rev. ed. (Ithaca, N.Y., 1966),
p. 17.
[31] Auerbach, p. 12.

is so much maligned, so often and so casually dismissed as a mode of mere feeling. It does, after all, restore feeling to its proper place in the creative experience. What is often overlooked, however, is that this proper place is not apart from imagery and intelligence and will. Poets no longer "thought and felt by fits, unbalanced." Poetry had become whole again. But, of course, this leaves us with a more difficult kind of poetry. It is generally less difficult to grasp the poetry of the eighteenth century. Thought and theme are clear, feeling is clear. We know how the poet wishes us to respond: we are told, in effect, to laugh, to weep, to feel pity. When thought and feeling are one, however, the task is more difficult. We are not told what to experience; we are simply led, by complex symbol, into the experience itself. There we find not merely an emotion, but also an experience of the poet's own self, of the mysteries of the world as the poet has experienced it, and perhaps our very selves.

Romanticism is often said to be marked by a new sense of freedom. This includes, of course, freedom as a theme— political, personal, philosophical, or religious; it includes freedom of literary structure, with the admission of a new openness of form; it includes freedom for the poet to express emotion in a more deeply personal way. But a freedom that has not often been noted is a freedom that comes precisely from the symbolic experience. It is the freedom given the reader by the poet. Since we are simply led into the experience—are not told, as in allegory or other poetry of fancy, what to experience—we are left free to be, perhaps to find, ourselves. It is a gift of no small moment.

But if the Romantic poetry of symbol gives us the blessing of freedom, this blessing is not without its price. This price is the willingness to live with mystery—the mysteries of the known and the unknown, of the finite and the infinite, of one's deepest self, of oneself and the other. In the end, symbol gives us, as it gives the poet, the terrible and beautiful freedom to encounter the mysteries of the human spirit.

8

Symbol and Religion:
Past and Future

THE PROBLEM of the symbolic forms of religious expression
has been a recurring theme in theology. Theologian John
Shea has written that

> when the traditional interpretive schemes of human existence
> are no longer emotionally and motivationally satisfying,
> when the inherited symbols have become opaque instead of
> sacramental, when religious language seems ossified instead
> of revelatory conversation, man returns to experience. Here
> he hopes to encounter the real in some primitive and urgent
> way and so reground his life. He wants to shed the cumber-
> some superstructures of thought which he believes have hard-
> ened rather than sharpened his sensibilities. He hopes to sink
> into his own experiences, explore them, listen to them.[1]

For this reason, some modern theologians have found
Coleridge of special value. For many contemporary theologians, the work of theology is not merely, or primarily, the
translation of the language of Scripture into the abstractions
of a scientific discourse, but also a process of discovery in
which religious experience is gradually unfolded; and since
the object of this experience is a transcendent God, there is
truly no end to the unfolding. Something of this (in Christian terms) is suggested by a remark by theologian David
Tracy: "The Christian focus on the event of Jesus Christ
discloses the always-already, not-yet reality of grace. That
grace, when reflected upon, unfolds its fuller meaning into
the ordered relationships of the God who is love, the world

---

[1] "Human Experience and Religious Symbolization." *The Ecumenist*,
9 (1971), 49.

that is beloved and a self gifted and commanded to become loving."[2] The object of the theological endeavor is not simply a past event, but also an ongoing encounter with the God who precipitated that event and who continues to make it operative in our lives. It is no accident that Tracy's remark is in a book on the imagination, in which he enunciates forcefully the need for an "analogical imagination" if the modern pluralistic tradition of theology is to flourish. The analogical imagination can allow the Christian theologian not only to continue "a journey into her/his own particularity, but also to be open to the riches of other religious and theological traditions."[3] Clearly for Tracy, as for Coleridge, the language in which one talks about the transcendent God must be able to encompass the reality of process and growth, because in the work of theology the quest for understanding is never done.

It is perhaps for this reason that so-called "narrative theology" has come into being, founded on the belief that, as James William McClendon, Jr. suggests, "narrative or *story* is a means of expression uniquely suited to theology or at least to Christian theology." McClendon concedes that "at first glance such claims seem radically at odds with traditional 'propositional' theology."[4] However, the attention being given in modern scholarship to the role of myth in religious expression, the increasing realization that story is inevitably a part of the religious tradition—whether it be Old Testament stories like that of Abraham and Isaac, the narrative sections of the Veda, the tales of Bantu storytellers or of Talmudic scholars, or the Christian gospels—have brought many theologians to consider more seriously the narrative dimension of the theological enterprise. Stephen Crites has even suggested that (in James McClendon's summary) "human experience necessarily has a narrative form. . . . the time-defying strategies of modern intellectual work

---

[2] *The Analogical Imagination: Christian Theology and the Culture of Pluralism* (New York, 1981), p. 446.

[3] Tracy, p. 449.

[4] *Biography as Theology: How Life Stories Can Remake Today's Theology* (Nashville, Tenn., 1974), p. 188.

(conceptual abstraction; phenomenological contraction of attention) cannot ever really overcome this necessary form, so that the 'sacred stories' by which primitive people live their lives, are representative of the dwelling places of all human beings; we all live in some 'story' or other."[5] Such a conception can encompass both the real that was and the ideal that is yet to be, drawing the reader/viewer/worshiper forward into the future, even as it makes present the mystery of the past.

If the problem of symbolic forms is very much in the minds of theologians of our age, it was equally so in the nineteenth century. Yet we find it formulated often enough not merely by theologians but by literary figures as well. There is a startling similarity, for example, between the lines just quoted and a passage from the *Autobiography of Mark Rutherford*, recording his youthful reading of the *Lyrical Ballads*. "It conveyed to me no new doctrine, and yet the change it wrought in me could only be compared with that which is said to have been wrought on Paul himself by the Divine apparition." Wordsworth would have been, he says, "the last man to say that he had lost his faith in the God of his fathers. But his real God is not the God of the Church, but the God of the hills." As a result of Wordsworth's influence,

> instead of an object of worship which was altogether artificial, remote, never coming into genuine contact with me, I had now one which I thought to be real, one in which literally I could live and move and have my being, an actual fact present before my eyes. God was brought from that heaven of the books, and dwelt on the downs in the far-away distances, and in every cloud-shadow which wandered across the valley. Wordsworth unconsciously did for me what every religious reformer has done,—he re-created my Supreme Divinity;

---

[5] McClendon, p. 189. For Crites's essay, "The Narrative Quality of Experience," see *Journal of the American Academy of Religion*, 39 (1971), 291–311.

substituting a new and living spirit for the old deity, once alive, but gradually hardened into an idol.[6]

It should come as no surprise that a theologian and a literary man should enunciate what is essentially the same problem—the hardening of religious forms and sensibilities—and offer essentially the same response: a return to human experience. For it may be suspected by now that the change we have seen in the mode of poetic perception and creation rests at bottom on a profound change in religious sensibility. The religious apprehension of reality is not apart from other human perceptions. All such perceptions function according to the laws of the human mind and imagination, all function within the limits of human language; and human language—to say nothing of an individual's mindset and the cast of his or her imagination—is constantly changing. What makes the change in religious sensibility particularly important is that it is here that language is most intensely strained, imagination most severely tested. It is religious apprehension and expression that most urgently demand both clarity and suggestiveness, because they are straining to embrace what is deeply one and yet remains not only "other," but ultimately transcendent, numinous, mysterious.

By the late eighteenth century the "inherited symbols," not only of religion but of poetry as well, had "become opaque instead of sacramental," and there was need of a new "sacramental" view of the poetic act to make these symbols once again (to use Coleridge's word) "translucent." Perhaps ironically, this opaqueness came from an excessive refinement in the expression of religious belief. We see it in every shade of belief and unbelief—in such an orthodox Christian apologist as Bishop Butler, in such a skeptic as Hume.

---

[6] William Hale White ("Mark Rutherford"), *The Autobiography of Mark Rutherford, Dissenting Minister* (2nd ed.; London, 1936), pp. 21–23.

For Hume, there was a kind of grossness about Christianity, an excess of humanity, that he found intolerable. Like so many others of his century, he could not abide mystery. The mystery of established religion is bound up, for him, with mankind's inability to image God except in human terms. God is always, by Hume's lights, too immersed in human concerns. God should be viewed more abstractly, distant from mankind, apart in splendid isolation. But if it is true that "humankind cannot bear very much reality," it is also true that humankind cannot focus for long on such an abstraction, however glorious, and so we construct mediators between God and ourselves, which become in effect idols, false gods. Theism should be allowed, Hume believed, only if it is free from primitivism, free from the grossness of mediators and sacraments, free from the distorted perceptions of common humanity, free from the darkness of mystery. As Basil Willey says, Hume might have pleaded, "Oh for a revelation! but not, if you please, the one we are supposed to have had already."[7] As it is, for Hume, as for much of the eighteenth century, a refined deism, devoted to the contemplation of an abstraction, would have to suffice.

Reactions to the deist position, found in such disparate orthodox divines as Bishop Butler and Archdeacon Paley, as well as in such less orthodox adherents of Christianity as Hartley and Priestley, are something less than fully responsive. It is true that, as Basil Willey points out, Bishop Butler "seems to discern the radical defect of eighteenth-century deism, namely that it makes man the measure of all things, and takes no account of the most significant elements of religious experience—those, namely, which involve an acknowledgment of paradox, even of irrationality at the heart of things, certainly of transcendence or 'otherness'; of God not merely as deified Reason but as *mysterium tremendum*" (pp. 83–84). However, Butler seems, no more than any of

---

[7] *The Eighteenth Century Background: Studies on the Idea of Nature in the Thought of the Period* (Boston, 1961), p. 135. See also pp. 126–135.

the others, to be able truly to respond to the issues they raise. Perhaps the problem lies in the choice of a field of combat; the Christian apologists chose, by and large—there was an occasional exception like William Law—to fight on the deists' own ground, reason. Paley's *Evidences of Christianity*, one of the most influential religious books of the late eighteenth century, falls of its own weight as it tries to prove what is ultimately unprovable, the truth of Christianity. Even Bishop Butler, a far more sophisticated thinker, relies heavily on the arguments of reason. Concerned primarily with God's governance of the world, both the natural and the moral orders, Butler responds in terms of law. There is an observable law of nature, implanted by the Creator, and a discernible law of conscience, written on human hearts. Both are given to mankind to show the way to God.

This is, surely, one of the central themes of eighteenth-century thought: God is to be found both in the world of nature—"the starry heavens"—and in the law within—the promptings of the human heart. But actually what is it that is to be found? It is commonly not so much God as the laws of God. What is found indwelling in nature is not God present, but the law of God's reason. What is found in "the heart of man" is not, as in traditional Christian theology, the indwelling Spirit of God, but the created law of conscience (to use Butler's word) or (in Hartley's phrases) "theopathy" and "the moral sense." God has left divine marks on creation but remains absent from it. These marks are often, one is tempted to say—in Gerard Manley Hopkins's words—"like dead letters sent / To dearest him that lives alas! away." In the view of many eighteenth-century apologists, the Christian is still almost as far from God as the deist is from Hume's "abstract Deity."[8]

---

[8] Of course, there were exceptions to the prevailing currents of thought and sensibility; there were forces counter not only to deistic rationalism but also to the rationalism of Christian apologists. The most important was the rise of Methodism. As Stephen Prickett says, there was in John Wesley "a renewed stress on the Incarnation—where God's immanence in nature is revealed." *Coleridge and Wordsworth: The Poetry of Growth* (Cambridge, 1970), p. 105. Methodism was in its beginnings much more

The differences among theologians and religious philosophers in the eighteenth century are as great as they are in
any age, of course, but three intertwining motifs recur insis-
tently, whether one is reading Shaftesbury or Hume, Hartley
or Butler, Priestley or Paley. The three motifs are closely
linked. First of all, the supernatural is effectively banished
from the world of nature; reason reigns supreme, and only
the natural can be truly apprehended. Then, there is the distaste for mystery—whether it be the mystery of sin, the
mystery of freedom, or the mystery in the conception of
God; mystery is beyond the grasp of reason and, therefore,
necessarily suspect. Finally, there is the conception of God
as the Divine Artificer, who looks on from a distance at the
created world. The net effect, clearly, is an evacuation of
the sense of the sacred, the numinous, the "other." It is a
loss of presence, a loss of the immanent presence of the
transcendent; and with this, there is a loss of the felt presence of mystery.

The eighteenth-century world-view is, of course, essentially scientific, an Enlightenment view. It is not only religious language that seems "ossified" discourse instead of
"revelatory conversation," but language itself—all the "inherited symbols"—that has "become opaque." The desire
of the Enlightenment, at least from the time of Locke, was
(as Robert Langbaum puts it) to "separate fact from the values of a crumbling tradition." In the process, however, it
"separated fact from all values—bequeathing a world in
which fact is measurable quantity while value is man-made
and illusory."[9]

---

a movement of popular religious sentiment than of poetic sensibility or
of theological reflection. Early on it did not seem to have touched very
deeply the intellectual or artistic life of the upper classes. It was not until
late in the century that Methodism began to influence poetry and theology
in any marked degree, and then it was in a poet like Blake, who in a real
sense belongs to a later age, an age of Romanticism. In spite of currents
to the contrary, the intellectual life of the eighteenth century remained
predominantly rationalist. On Wesley and Methodism, see Gerald R.
Cragg, *Reason and Authority in the Eighteenth Century* (Cambridge,
1964), pp. 155–180.

[9] *The Poetry of Experience* (New York, 1963), p. 11.

Yet whatever the philosophers and theologians—and sometimes the poets—may write, human beings do experience values, very much including the presence of mystery. There is precisely the rub. There is a gap between the writings of philosophers and poets, and people's daily lives. "Such a world," Langbaum says, "offers no objective verification for just the perceptions by which men live, perceptions of beauty, goodness and spirit" (p. 11)—the perceptions of mystery. The inherited symbols have become opaque; there is a divorce between language and experience.

The answer could only be a return from the abstract to the concrete—what John Stuart Mill conceived of as the replacement of the Lockean tradition by the teaching of Coleridge—a return from abstract idea to concrete experience. What was needed was a new trust in the wholeness of human experience and in the language by which we express experience. Only by such an act of trust, admittedly a kind of act of faith, could human beings accept the fact that the objectively verifiable does not exhaust the range of human experience. Hence, the need for symbol, which can express not only what is objectively verifiable—the material of science—but also what finds its only verification in our willing and feeling encounter with it—the subjective, the ideal, and the sacred. Robert Langbaum is pointing to this same need when he remarks that Romanticism—the response to this need—is "both idealistic and realistic in that it conceives of the ideal as existing only in conjunction with the real and the real as existing only in conjunction with the ideal. The two are brought into conjunction only in the act of perception when the higher or imaginative rationality brings the ideal to the real by penetrating and possessing the external world as a way of knowing both itself and the external world" (p. 24). What poets begin to strive for is a "simultaneity of word and experience" (p. 69), which (I would add) involves at the same time a simultaneous apprehension of fact and value. When this simultaneity is achieved, the opaqueness of language disappears and is replaced by the translucence of symbol. In symbol, language and experience, sign and thing signified, fact and value, are grasped together—lit by a single light—seen in and through each other. The several realities—real and ideal, particular and universal, self and other, concrete and numinous—are apprehended together in a single vision.

It was some time before the return to the wholeness of human experience began to touch theology deeply. Paley's rationalistic *Evidences*, for example, remained the canonical university text on apologetics well into the nineteenth century; and Newman's *Grammar of Assent*, with its famous distinction between notional and real assent, did not appear until 1870. Coleridge, though a solitary voice in his generation, did begin the task, with *The Statesman's Manual*, *Aids to Reflection*, and *On the Constitution of the Church and the State*, all predicated on the need for symbol, a medium between the literal and the merely metaphorical. He at least began the work—to be continued by thinkers like Newman, J. C. Hare, and F. D. Maurice—of returning theological reflection from the realm of abstract speculation to the world of human experience.

Poetry, fortunately, did not have to wait so long. With Wordsworth and Coleridge, the "poetry of experience" was not only well begun but already brought to crowning achievement. As we have seen, poetry was no longer merely pointing at things, setting side by side the real and the ideal, the object and the self, the concrete and the numinous, hoping that they would somehow touch each other. Poetry was achieving singleness of vision, perceiving disparate realities—the object and the self, even the secular and the sacred—in translucent symbol. The oneness of these realities, seen as consubstantial with each other, could now be sensed, could be felt along the heart, could be glimpsed at least out of the corner of the eye, and sometimes even seen in steady if mysterious vision.

We have said that it was a change in religious sensibility that underlies this change in poetic sensibility. One might be tempted to say that what is central to this change is a new release of feeling, that emotion has been newly admitted into the expression of religious experience, in response to eighteenth-century rationalism. Surely, this is part of the answer, as Methodism began to encourage the release of emotion in public and private worship. But the deepest change is, rather, to be found in three new, deeply interrelated viewpoints, all of which have been adumbrated in the course of this book.

First of all, there is a renewed admission of the role of the human will in religious experience, allowing the possibility of a free commitment of the self in faith, a trusting encounter with the real in whatever way it is experienced—not only when it is "objectively verifiable." With this there is a new willingness to live in mystery. The real that is encountered need not be quantifiable or classifiable; it may even partially transcend our human powers of comprehension. Finally, there is a renewed perception of the oneness—Coleridge's consubstantiality—of all being. It is possible, therefore, to speak meaningfully of the numinous—whether it be the transcendent deity, the immanent presence of the divine in nature, or the sacred glimpsed in the depths of oneself—by true analogy with sensible reality. No longer is the sacred awesomely apart; it is awesomely present. The numinous that is glimpsed in our natural and human worlds ("quick now, here, now, always") gives true, if limited, reports of an ideal, transcendent reality. More than that, it is itself experience of that reality.

In longer perspective, this change in religious sensibility is only a moment in a whole history of change. J. Hillis Miller begins his study of the "disappearance of God" in five nineteenth-century writers with the pre-Socratic philosophers and the earliest writings of the Old Testament, where the divine power was experienced as "immediately present in nature, in society, and in each man's heart. So Moses saw God in the burning bush, and so Parmenides and Heraclitus are philosopher-poets of total immanence."[10] Symbols were

---

[10] *The Disappearance of God: Five Nineteenth-Century Writers* (New York, 1965), pp. 2–3.

not apart from the realities they represented. "Poetry was meaningful in the same way as nature itself—by a communion of the verbal symbols with the reality they named." This sacramental sense already present in Western culture was ratified and strengthened, in Miller's view, by the Incarnation of Christ and by the Eucharist, "the manifestation and guarantee of communion" (p. 3).

"The history of modern literature," on the other hand—and by this Miller means roughly from the seventeenth century on—"is in part the history of the splitting apart of this communion" (p. 3). One might not care to link this change quite so closely as he does with the Protestant view of the Eucharist (especially the Zwinglian or Calvinistic view of the Eucharist as, in Miller's phrase, "the expression of an absence" rather than a presence), but the diminishing of a sacramental sense in theology is at least a striking parallel to the changes in literature. It is not only things themselves but words as well that have lost their sacramental dimension. Verlaine's poetry of pure music ("de la musique avant toute chose") is only the inevitable climax of a long history. Miller continues: "In this evolution words have been gradually hollowed out, and have lost their substantial participation in material or spiritual reality" (p. 6). Modernity in literature expresses a sense of loss, of isolation. Men and women are separated from nature, from other people, and from God. "Modern thought has been dominated by the presupposition that each man is locked in the prison of his consciousness. From Montaigne to Descartes and Locke, on down through associationism, idealism, and romanticism to the phenomenology and existentialism of today, the assumption has been that man must start with the inner experience of the isolated self" (p. 8).

Up to this point I can only agree, but I am brought up short by the proposition that "in all the stages of modern thought the interior states of the self are a beginning which in some sense can never be transcended" (p. 8). However valid Miller's account may be for some figures of the later nineteenth century—as I believe it is also by and large for

the eighteenth century—it falls seriously short of account-
ing for the phenomenon of Romanticism. Miller portrays
the Romantic artist as at bottom an idealist, "the man who
in the absence of a given world must create his own. The
central assumption of romanticism is the idea that the isolated individual, through poetry, can . . . create through his
own efforts a marvelous harmony of words which will inte-
grate man, nature, and God." What we have been arguing
throughout about Coleridge, the central theorist of Romanticism, is that his theory and use of symbol (as well as Wordsworth's) has allowed him to escape from the trap of pure
idealism, and we have suggested that the same is true generally of the other Romantics. Coleridge's borrowings from
the German idealists helped him to articulate his own subjective experience, but he was able, by the openness of his
symbol to all reality, to transmute this idealism into a
healthy realism—ideal yet real, personalist yet not solipsis-
tic. Romantic theory is predicated not simply on creation
but on imaginative re-creation, the poet's subjective ordering responding to an order of things at least sensed in the
reality outside him.

What Miller says of the centrality of the loss of the sacramental sense in literature since the end of the seventeenth
century rings true. There is a sense of loss, of isolation;
there is, in some measure, a withdrawal of the sacred—
including a "disappearance of God." But the Romantic
spirit is, to my mind, a notable exception to this otherwise
fairly linear development. In its sense of the presence of the
divine in the world, Romanticism is at least a moment's return to an earlier view of the world. What still remains to us
of this Romantic spirit may be, in fact, one of literature's
last real holds on the objective real.

Romanticism does not just happen and then disappear. We
have come to see in recent decades that what we call "Romanticism" may be an element present, in greater or less
degree, in every period and in every work of art. Earlier
views (like that, for example, of Friedrich Schlegel) tended
to see Classic and Romantic as two mutually antagonistic

modes of artistic expression. We can see now, however, that (as art historian Eric Newton puts it) they are really "two different attitudes of mind, each capable of enriching the other when fused together—each, indeed, producing an impoverished element when isolated. What makes Bach greater than his contemporaries is his unexpected moments of mystery and nostalgia. What makes Wagner immortal is the formal pattern that underlies his magnificent hysteria."[11] An age is called Classic or Romantic not because it is totally one or the other, but because the tendency of an age is commonly in the direction either of objectivity and finished, formal perfection, or of subjectivity and the open-endedness of questioning and mystery. Great art will never be wholly one or the other. Even Pope reveals the energy of feeling, however restrained; even Wordsworth, however far from Milton, is undergirded by the sinewy strength of a rhythmic line and some of the structural patterns of epic form. There is in all great art a Coleridgean "reconciliation of opposites."

The question remains, as it probably always will, of what constitutes the Romantic element of art. We have been warned, ever since Lovejoy's famous essay of 1923, to "discriminate Romanticisms." But the search goes on, at least sporadically, for definition. Perhaps this is where symbol can come fruitfully into play, allowing a definition that does not define so narrowly as to distort the significance of the many Romanticisms we find. There is one Romanticism, like that of the "Ancient Mariner," characterized by a sense of human weakness, isolation, and incompleteness; another exalts the human will, like Manfred's, to the level of divinity. A Romanticism like Sir Walter Scott's looks backward in a cult of the past, especially the medieval past; another, like Wordsworth's, tends to look forward to a hopeful, even paradisal, future. There is a primitivist Romanticism that elevates nature above art, simplicity above complexity; another that is not primitive but highly sophisticated, necessarily artful by reason of its very complexity. The word

---

[11] *The Romantic Rebellion* (New York, 1964), p. 12.

"Romanticism" has been applied to so many things that many critics have despaired of it.

Yet it may be that there is a common element in all these Romanticisms—the element of mystery. Whether it be a romanticized past or an idealized future of infinite progress; a sense of isolation and insecurity or a sense of god-like power; the simplicities of primal and primitive nature or the complexities of an art that tries to embrace as much reality as possible—there is always mystery. Wherever one finds Romanticism one finds mystery; and wherever one finds mystery one will find symbol, for only symbol can represent and, however imperfectly, articulate mystery.

It is for this reason that there will always be a Romantic spirit, however attenuated, in every age. There are ages that, like the age of Pope, tend to subordinate the element of mystery to the very real clarities that can be achieved— whether they be clarities of social mores or of political life. There are other ages that, like the early nineteenth century in England, are driven—by political and historical influences, by reaction to (in W. Jackson Bate's phrase) "the burden of the past," or by simple human need—to face the mysteries more squarely. And there are the ages between, like the later eighteenth century, that are only beginning to feel the need for a more intense experience and articulation of the human mysteries.

We have made, at least implicitly, rather sweeping claims for Romantic symbol, suggesting that symbol is able to achieve a greater grasp of reality than other forms of poetic expression. In particular, the claim has been made—and, I hope, substantiated by soundings in the poetry of symbolic encounter—that it is only through symbol that the poet can articulate the transcendent, even the numinous, in human experience. It is one of the characteristics of Romanticism, in whatever form it may be found, that it conveys a sense of two worlds. The Romantic temper is commonly characterized, as Professor Lovejoy says, by "a revolt against naturalism," by "an ethical and metaphysical dualism, a philosophy of two worlds." [12] This is not to say that the Classical spirit is necessarily not religious. The point is, rather, that the Classical temper, even when it admits of a world of numinous or transcendent values, does not see it closely interacting with the world of everyday reality and everyday action; ethical values tend to be determined by humanistic norms, with humankind as the measure; higher metaphysical and religious values may exist, but they exist in a world apart. The sacred, the numinous, the transcendent, are not present but in a world elsewhere; they are pointed to, but they are not encountered. There is no great need for symbol in such a world-view, for there is no need to express the mystery of two interacting worlds. In the Romantic view, however, these two worlds—each present to the other, each consubstantial with the other—can and must be embraced by the translucence of symbol, in which both worlds can be seen in the light of a single vision.

Let there be no mistake. The symbol of which Coleridge wrote—and which he used—is not simply "religious" in some narrow sense. It may indeed express the transcendent in human experience, but it may be as well the vehicle for the expression of what we have called the sacred in the depths of the self. For the symbolic poet the two experiences are commonly not separate. Humankind will always grope to articulate the "ground of being," wherever it is to be found, and symbol will be the vehicle of that expression. As there will always be such a striving, in greater or less degree, there will always be in some measure a Romantic temper, and there will always be a symbolic element in the most profound of our poetry. It is for this reason that the Romantic spirit lives on, though rising and falling in importance from age to age—not so much through literary influence, though lines of influence can be drawn, as through the perennially questing human mind and heart.

---

[12] "Coleridge and Kant's Two Worlds," *Essays in the History of Ideas* (Baltimore, 1948), p. 275.

LIST OF WORKS CITED

Abrams, M. H. "Coleridge's 'A Light in Sound': Science, Metascience, and Poetic Imagination." *Proceedings of the American Philosophical Society*, 116 (1972), 458–476.

―――. *Natural Supernaturalism: Tradition and Revolution in Romantic Literature*. New York: W. W. Norton, 1971.

Appleyard, J. A., S.J. *Coleridge's Philosophy of Literature: The Development of a Concept of Poetry, 1791–1819*. Cambridge, Mass.: Harvard University Press, 1965.

Auerbach, Erich. *Mimesis: The Representation of Reality in Western Literature*. Princeton: Princeton University Press, 1953.

Baker, James Volant. *The Sacred River: Coleridge's Theory of the Imagination*. Baton Rouge, La.: Louisiana State University Press, 1957.

Barfield, Owen. *What Coleridge Thought*. Middletown, Conn.: Wesleyan University Press, 1971.

Barth, J. Robert, S.J. *Coleridge and Christian Doctrine*. Cambridge, Mass.: Harvard University Press, 1969. Repr. New York: Fordham University Press, 1987.

―――, and John L. Mahoney, eds. *Coleridge, Keats, and the Imagination: Romanticism and Adam's Dream*. Columbia, Mo.: University of Missouri Press, 1990.

Bate, W. Jackson. *The Burden of the Past and the English Poet*. Cambridge, Mass.: Harvard University Press, Belknap Press, 1970.

Boulger, James D. "Coleridge on the Imagination Revisited." *The Wordsworth Circle*, 4 (1973), 13–24.

Carlyle, Thomas. *Sartor Resartus: The Life and Opinions of Herr Teufelsdröckh*. Ed. Charles Frederick Harrold. Garden City, N.Y.: Doubleday, 1937.

Cohen, Ralph. *The Unfolding of "The Seasons."* Baltimore: The Johns Hopkins University Press, 1970.

Coleridge, Samuel Taylor. *Aids to Reflection.* Ed. John Beer, in *The Collected Works*, ed. Coburn, IX. Princeton: Princeton University Press, 1993.

————. *Biographia Literaria.* Ed. Henry Nelson Coleridge (completed by Sara Coleridge), in *The Complete Works*, ed. Shedd, III.

————. *Biographia Literaria.* Ed. James Engell and W. Jackson Bate, in *The Collected Works*, ed. Coburn, VII. 2 vols. Princeton: Princeton University Press, 1983.

————. *Biographia Literaria.* Ed. John Shawcross. 2 vols. Oxford: Oxford University Press, 1907.

————. *Collected Letters of Samuel Taylor Coleridge.* Ed. Earl Leslie Griggs. 6 vols. Oxford: Clarendon Press, 1956–1971.

————. *The Collected Works of Samuel Taylor Coleridge.* Ed. Kathleen Coburn. Bollingen Series 75. Princeton: Princeton University Press, 1969–.

————. *The Complete Poetical Works of Samuel Taylor Coleridge.* Ed. Ernest Hartley Coleridge. 2 vols. Oxford: Clarendon Press, 1912.

————. *The Complete Works of Samuel Taylor Coleridge, with an Introductory Essay upon His Philosophical and Theological Opinions.* Ed. W. G. T. Shedd. 7 vols. New York: Harper and Brothers, 1856.

————. *The Friend: A Series of Essays to Aid in the Formation of Fixed Principles in Politics, Morals, and Religion, with Literary Amusements Interspersed.* Ed. Barbara E. Rooke, in *The Collected Works*, ed. Coburn, IV. 2 vols. Princeton: Princeton University Press, 1969.

————. *Inquiring Spirit.* Ed. Kathleen Coburn. London: Routledge and Kegan Paul, 1951.

————. *Lay Sermons.* Ed. R. J. White, in *The Collected Works*, ed. Coburn, VI. Princeton: Princeton University Press, 1972.

————. *Lectures 1808–1819 On Literature.* Ed. R. A.

Foakes, in *The Collected Works*, ed. Coburn, V. 2 vols. Princeton: Princeton University Press, 1987.

————. *The Literary Remains of Samuel Taylor Coleridge*. Ed. Henry Nelson Coleridge. 4 vols. London: W. Pickering, 1836–1839.

————. *Coleridge's Miscellaneous Criticism*. Ed. Thomas Middleton Raysor. 2 vols. Cambridge, Mass.: Harvard University Press, 1936.

————. *The Notebooks of Samuel Taylor Coleridge*. Ed. Kathleen Coburn. 4 vols. to date. Bollingen Series 50. Princeton: Princeton University Press, 1955–.

————. *The Philosophical Lectures of Samuel Taylor Coleridge*. Ed. Kathleen Coburn. New York: Philosophical Library, 1949.

————. *The Poetical Works of Samuel Taylor Coleridge*. Ed. James Dykes Campbell. London: Macmillan, 1893.

————. *Shakespearean Criticism*. Ed. Thomas Middleton Raysor. 2 vols. London: J. M. Dent, Everyman's Library, 1960.

————. *Table Talk*. Ed. Carl Woodring, in *The Collected Works*, ed. Coburn, XIV. 2 vols. Princeton: Princeton University Press, 1990.

————, and William Wordsworth. See Wordsworth, William.

Coulson, John. *Newman and the Common Tradition: A Study in the Language of Church and Society*. Oxford: Clarendon Press, 1970.

Cowper, William. *Cowper: Verse and Letters*. Ed. Brian Spiller. Cambridge, Mass: Harvard University Press, 1968.

Cragg, Gerald R. *Reason and Authority in the Eighteenth Century*. Cambridge: Cambridge University Press, 1964.

Crane, Ronald S., ed. *A Collection of English Poems, 1660–1800*. New York: Harper & Row, 1932.

Crites, Stephen. "The Narrative Quality of Experience." *Journal of the American Academy of Religion*, 39 (1971), 291–311.

Cutsinger, James. "Coleridgean Polarity and Theological

Vision." *Harvard Theological Review*, 76 (1983), 91–108.

———. *The Form of Transformed Vision: Coleridge and the Knowledge of God*. Macon, Ga.: Mercer University Press, 1987.

Dryden, John. *Prose 1668–1691, Essay of Dramatick Poesie and Shorter Works*. Ed. Samuel Holt Monk, in *The Works of John Dryden*, ed. Edward Niles Hooker and H. T. Swedenberg, XVII. Berkeley: University of California Press, 1971.

Eliot, T. S. *Selected Essays*. New York: Harcourt, Brace, 1932.

Engell, James. *The Creative Imagination: Enlightenment to Romanticism*. Cambridge, Mass.: Harvard University Press, 1981.

Feidelson, Charles, Jr. *Symbolism and American Literature*. Chicago: The University of Chicago Press, Phoenix Books, 1953.

Fogle, Richard Harter. *The Idea of Coleridge's Criticism*. Perspectives in Criticism 9. Berkeley: University of California Press, 1962.

Gallant, Christine, ed. *Coleridge's Theory of Imagination Today*. New York: AMS Press, 1989.

Garber, Frederick. *Wordsworth and the Poetry of Encounter*. Urbana, Ill.: University of Illinois Press, 1971.

Happel, Stephen. *Coleridge's Religious Imagination*. Salzburg Studies in English Literature. 3 vols. Salzburg: Institut für Anglistik und Americanistik, 1983.

Harding, Anthony John. *Coleridge and the Inspired Word*. Kingston: McGill-Queen's University Press, 1985.

———. "Imagination, Patriarchy, and Evil in Coleridge and Heidegger." *Studies in Romanticism*, 35 (1996), 3–26.

Haven, Richard. *Patterns of Consciousness: An Essay on Coleridge*. Amherst, Mass.: The University of Massachusetts Press, 1969.

Honig, Edwin. *Dark Conceit: The Making of Allegory*. New York: Oxford University Press, Galaxy Books, 1966.

House, Humphry. *Coleridge: The Clark Lectures, 1951–52.* London: Rupert Hart-Davis, 1953.

Kahler, Erich. "The Nature of the Symbol." *Symbolism in Religion and Literature,* ed. Rollo May. New York: George Braziller, 1960. Pp. 50–74.

Knights, L. C. "Idea and Symbol: Some Hints from Coleridge." *Coleridge: A Collection of Critical Essays,* ed. Kathleen Coburn. Englewood Cliffs, N.J.: Prentice-Hall, 1967. Pp. 112–122.

Langbaum, Robert. *The Poetry of Experience.* The Norton Library. New York: W. W. Norton, 1963.

Lewis, C. S. *The Allegory of Love: A Study in Medieval Tradition.* New York: Oxford University Press, Galaxy Books, 1959.

Lipkowitz, Ina. "Inspiration and Poetic Imagination: Samuel Taylor Coleridge." *Studies in Romanticism,* 30 (1991), 605–631.

Lonergan, Bernard, S.J., *Divinarum Personarum Conceptio Analogica.* Rome: Pontificia Universitas Gregoriana, 1957.

Lovejoy, Arthur O. "Coleridge and Kant's Two Worlds." *Essays in the History of Ideas.* Baltimore: The Johns Hopkins University Press, 1948.

McClendon, James William, Jr. *Biography as Theology: How Life Stories Can Remake Today's Theology.* Nashville, Tenn.: Abingdon Press, 1974.

McFarland, Thomas P. "Involute and Symbol in the Romantic Imagination." Barth and Mahoney, 29–57.

———. *Originality and Imagination.* Baltimore: The Johns Hopkins University Press, 1985.

———. "The Symbiosis of Coleridge and Wordsworth." *Studies in Romanticism,* 11 (1972), 263–303.

Miller, J. Hillis. *The Disappearance of God: Five Nineteenth-Century Writers.* New York: Schocken Books, 1965.

Newton, Eric. *The Romantic Rebellion.* New York: Schocken Books, 1964.

Perkins, David, ed. *English Romantic Writers*. New York: Harcourt, Brace, and World, 1967.

———. *The Quest for Permanence: The Symbolism of Wordsworth, Shelley, and Keats*. Cambridge, Mass.: Harvard University Press, 1959.

Perkins, Mary Anne. *Coleridge's Philosophy: The Logos as Unifying Principle*. Oxford: Clarendon Press, 1994.

Perry, Seamus. *Coleridge and the Uses of Division*. Oxford: Clarendon Press, 1999.

Politzer, Heinz. *Franz Kafka: Parable and Paradox*. Rev. ed. Ithaca, N.Y.: Cornell University Press, Cornell Paperbacks, 1966.

Prickett, Stephen. *Coleridge and Wordsworth: The Poetry of Growth*. Cambridge: Cambridge University Press, 1970.

———. *Words and the Word: Language, Poetics and Biblical Interpretation*. Cambridge: Cambridge University Press, 1986.

Reid, Nicholas. "The Satanic Principle in the Later Coleridge's Theory of Imagination." *Studies in Romanticism*, 37 (1998), 259–277.

Richards, I. A. *Coleridge on Imagination*. Bloomington, Ind.: Indiana University Press, Midland Books, 1960.

Schillebeeckx, Edouard, O.P. *Christ the Sacrament of the Encounter with God*. New York: Sheed and Ward, 1963.

Shea, John. "Human Experience and Religious Symbolization." *The Ecumenist*, 9 (1971), 49–52.

Spacks, Patricia Meyer. *The Poetry of Vision: Five Eighteenth Century Poets*. Cambridge, Mass.: Harvard University Press, 1967.

Swiatecka, Jadwiga. *The Idea of the Symbol: Some Nineteenth-Century Comparisons with Coleridge*. Cambridge: Cambridge University Press, 1980.

Tennyson, G. B. *"Sartor" Called "Resartus."* Princeton: Princeton University Press, 1965.

Tillich, Paul. *Dynamics of Faith*. World Perspectives 10. New York: Harper, 1956.

Todorov, Tzvetan. *Theories of the Symbol*. Trans. Catherine Porter. Ithaca, N.Y.: Cornell University Press, 1982.

Tracy, David. *The Analogical Imagination: Christian Theology and the Culture of Pluralism*. New York: Crossroad, 1981.

Unterecker, John. *A Reader's Guide to William Butler Yeats*. New York: Farrar, Straus & Company, Noonday Press, 1959.

Wallace, Catherine Miles. *The Design of Biographia Literaria*. London: George Allen and Unwin, 1983.

Warren, Robert Penn. *Selected Essays*. New York: Vintage Books, 1958.

Watson, George. *Coleridge the Poet*. London: Routledge and Kegan Paul, 1966.

Watson, Jeanie. *Risking Enchantment: Coleridge's Symbolic World of Faery*. Lincoln, Neb.: University of Nebraska Press, 1990.

Wendling, Ronald C. "Coleridge and the Consistency of 'The Eolian Harp'." *Studies in Romanticism*, 8 (1968), 26–42.

———. *Coleridge's Progress to Christianity: Experience and Authority in Religious Faith*. Lewisburg, Pa.: Bucknell University Press, 1995.

White, William Hale ("Mark Rutherford"). *The Autobiography of Mark Rutherford, Dissenting Minister*. 2nd ed. London: Oxford University Press, 1936.

Willey, Basil. *The Eighteenth Century Background: Studies on the Idea of Nature in the Thought of the Period*. Boston: Beacon Press, 1961.

Wordsworth, Jonathan. "The Infinite I AM: Coleridge and the Ascent of Being." *Coleridge's Imagination: Essays in Memory of Pete Laver*. Ed. Richard Gravil, Lucy Newlyn and Nicholas Roe. Cambridge: Cambridge University Press, 1985. Pp. 22–52.

Wordsworth, William. *The Cornell Wordsworth*. Ed. Stephen Parrish. Ithaca, N.Y.: Cornell University Press, 1975–.

———. *The Fourteen-Book Prelude*. Ed. W. J. B. Owen, in

The Cornell Wordsworth, ed. Stephen Parrish. Ithaca, N.Y.: Cornell University Press, 1985.

―――. *Literary Criticism of William Wordsworth.* Ed. Paul M. Zall. Regents Critics Series. Lincoln, Neb.: University of Nebraska Press, 1966.

―――. *The Thirteen-Book Prelude.* Ed. Mark L. Reed, in *The Cornell Wordsworth,* ed. Stephen Parrish. Ithaca, N.Y.: Cornell University Press, 1991.

―――. *Wordsworth: Poetical Works.* Ed. Thomas Hutchinson, rev. by Ernest de Selincourt. London: Oxford University Press, 1950.

―――, and Samuel Taylor Coleridge. *Lyrical Ballads: The Text of the 1798 Edition with the Additional 1800 Poems and the Prefaces.* Ed. R. L. Brett and A. R. Jones. London: Methuen, 1963.

INDEX

Kant, Immanuel, 7, 13, 140; his
views on subjectivity distinguished from Coleridge's,
135–137
Keats, John, 142
Knights, L. C., 145

Langbaum, Robert, 156–157
Law, William, 155
Lewis, C. S., 138–139
Lipkowitz, Ina, 14–15
Locke, John, 3, 156–157, 160
Lockridge, Laurence, 8
Logos, 12–13, 14; as primal sacra-
ment, 30
Lonergan, Bernard, 26, 29
Lovejoy, Arthur O., 162, 163–164
Lowth, Robert, 27n

Magnuson, Paul, 8
Mann, Thomas, 35
matrimony, 39, 43
Maurice, F. D., 158
McFarland, Thomas, 5–6, 8, 11–12,
96
Melville, Herman, 130
metaphor, distinguished from sym-
bol, 31–33, 53–58 passim; interac-
tion with symbol, 76–95 passim,
97–105 passim; metaphor/symbol
distinction related to fancy/imagi-
nation distinction, 76–95
Methodism, 155–156n, 159
Mileur, Jean-Pierre, 9
Mill, John Stuart, 157
Miller, J. Hillis, 159–161
Milton, John, 46, 51, 63, 101, 162
Modiano, Raimonda, 9
Montaigne, Michel de, 160

Newman, John Henry, 2, 27n, 158
Newton, Eric, 162
Nicaea, Council of, 37, 114
numinous, expressed by symbol,
143–148. See also transcendent

Paley, William, 154–155, 156, 158
pantheism, 8, 28
parable, 60
Parmenides, 159

Paul, St., 5, 36
Perkins, David, 91
Perkins, Mary Anne, 12–13
Perry, Seamus, 16–17
Plato, 5, 135–136, 138
Poe, Edgar Allan, 130
Politzer, Heinz, 148
Pope, Alexander, 47–49, 61, 62, 64,
162, 163
Prickett, Stephen, 27n, 155n
Priestley, Joseph, 154, 156

reason, distinguished from understanding, chap. 6 passim
Reid, Nicholas, 15–16
Richards, I. A., 29, 78, 113
romanticism, related to symbol,
161–164; religious characteristics,
163–164
"Rutherford, Mark" (William Hale
White), 152–153

sacrament, nature of, 39–40; as encounter, 40–46; sacramental vision in "The Rime of the Ancient
Mariner," 108–111; related to
symbol, 138–139, 142–145, 153;
sacramental sense in literature,
160–161
Schelling, Friedrich Wilhelm Joseph
von, 7, 13, 15, 33n, 140
Schillebeeckx, Edouard, 40–41
Schlegel, A. W., 33n
Schlegel, Friedrich von, 161
Scott, Sir Walter, 162
Scripture, symbol related to scrip-
tural mode of expression, 14–15,
145–148; related to imagination,
14–15, chap. 6 passim; symbol in,
31–32, 34
Shaftesbury, Anthony Ashley Coo-
per, third Earl of, 156
Shakespeare, William, 27, 35, 45,
48–51 passim, 56, 80, 123n; *King
Lear*, 78–79; *Venus and Adonis*,
78–79
Shawcross, J., 38n
Shea, John, 150
Shelley, Percy Bysshe, 142
Simpson, David, 9
Smart, Christopher, 61